The Ten Laws of Winning

The Secret to Living a Successful
and Productive Life.

by

DR. ADRIANNE AND OVETT WILSON

Watersprings
PUBLISHING

The Ten Laws Of Winning
Published by Watersprings Publishing, a division of
Watersprings Media House, LLC.
P.O. Box 1284
Olive Branch, MS 38654
www.waterspringsmedia.com
Contact publisher for bulk orders and permission requests.

Printed in the United States of America.

Library of Congress Control Number: 2020905143

ISBN-13: 978-1-948877-55-8

Table of Contents

The Ten Laws of Winning is dedicated to

Our parents, Millicent, Kenneth, Gloria and Jimmy,
thank you for teaching us how to win.
Your love and support are never-ending.

To our siblings, Roy, Anthony, Ann Marie, Floyd,
Jimmy, and Bryan, thank you for being a part
of our winning circle.

To our sons Jadon and Josiah,
may you always win in life.

Praises for
The Ten Laws of Winning

"I did not realize how much I needed this book until I read it. It addresses some key actions we can all take to overcome the obstacles holding us back from success. Not only is it inspirational but extremely practical. This book is like having a coach by your side. Read it if you are ready to win in life."
– Kymone Hinds, Ideas to Life CEO

"If you want a clear-cut method to winning, then this book is a must-read! It is jammed packed with knowledge and tools to help individuals establish a winner's mind-set."
– Jimmy Hall, Jr., United States Army, Sergeant Major

"Winning is an art and science. Dr. and Mr. Wilson provide a thorough blueprint for winning with this book! It is packed with the tools needed to establish a winning mentality!"
– Fred Reid, Toronto Argonauts Football Running Back Coach

"Wow! This book is powerful, captivating, and easy to read. It's filled with wisdom, practical advice, and rooted in research. It will change the way you approach life, your work, and the world. We all want to win."
– Dr. Rebecca Brown, M.D.

The "Ten Laws of Winning" provides key ingredients for success that are applicable to all organizations. As an administrator in a school district, the laws, if followed, can have amazing results for leaders, teachers, and students. The guiding questions that are included are a powerful tool to enhance individuals determined to achieve success alone or as part of a team.

– Dr. Yinka Alege, Principal Supervisor,
Hillsborough County Public Schools

"This book is thought-provoking, enjoyable, and easy to read. I highly recommend this book for anyone who is looking to tap into their winning spirit and gain more out of life!"

– Monica Davidson, Author of *Character Is Key To Success*

Foreword

As a Senior Non-Commissioned Officer (NCO) in the United States Navy, the concept of winning is embodied as early as boot camp. The very completion of boot camp is the first official act of winning. Winning is a way of life in the military. Every rank, promotion, or award serves as a monumental accomplishment. *The Ten Laws Of Winning* is no exception when it comes to understanding the fundamentals of success. This book gives anecdotal references as to what it takes to succeed and a clear battleplan to make it happen.

As explained thoroughly in this book, winning requires reverse engineering, which involves considering the victory before you even execute the plan. The Ten Laws provide a deep dive into the psychology associated with success, understanding the opposition, and how to eliminate distractions. The authors weave and thread the proverbial needle, touching every facet of our lives as it relates to being successful. *The Ten Laws Of Winning* makes for a great gift to every and anyone who has any doubt within themselves as to what is necessary in order to be great.

The mechanics involved in winning are beautifully captured in this book and to cite a quote:

> *"When we win, we usually do not immediately think about the process we undergo to make such victories a reality. However, the process is just as much, if not, more important than the victory itself."*

Often, the victory becomes the focus and not the hard work needed behind the scenes.

The authors create an easy to navigate roadmap of what it takes to win. This literary work is not linguistic gymnastics by any stretch of the imagination. As a verb, winning is grounded in action and the authors guide their readers to examine the rudiments of it. Authors, Ovett and Adrianne Wilson, are two educators who have worked tirelessly in the educational system, from elementary, middle, high, and college-level institutions. They've turned around programs and schools and are true winners within their own right.

As a Senior Chief Petty Officer in the United States Navy, winning translates to mission success; however, there is extensive preparatory work involved behind the scenes before anything happens. From the training of personnel, conducting preventative maintenance (PM) on equipment and machinery, personal development for advancement, or simply getting your uniform squared away. Each task, no matter how big or small, involves planning, knowledge, wisdom and understanding to execute.

Finally, as Americans, we love our sports teams, we buy, and wear replica jerseys and we even sometimes take on the personality of our favorite athlete. What do they all have in common? They are winners. They all have an intended outcome, understand their true north, and embrace their goals with a laser-focus clarity to win. I trust you will be truly inspired to share this work with others, and you will be so moved to embrace and apply The Ten Laws Of Winning into your daily life practices.

Roy Cunningham, *Senior Non-Commissioned Officer,*
United States Navy

INTRODUCTION

We All Like To Win

Everyone likes to win. Winning has an innate, nostalgic feeling to it, and many people enjoy the emotions associated with coming out on top. No one likes the idea of losing. Growing up, many days were spent trying to win. Winning is defined as gaining the desired result, or as achieving victory. A desired outcome of success is what many seek after. When we win, we usually do not immediately think of the process we undergo to make such victories a reality. However, the process is just as much, if not more important than the victory itself.

If we were to focus on the process of winning, the likelihood of duplicating victories would be that much higher. When you think of a winning program, team, company, or school, you must ask the question, why are they successful? What do they do? How do they do it? What makes them so different from the others? If being a winner was easy, everyone would be doing it. However, there is a process to having a winning spirit and that process has different internal and external aspects. The irony is that sometimes these processes aren't so enjoyable and may come with substantial fear and doubt, causing one to feel that their deliberate efforts won't support their desired victories.

Knowledge, Wisdom, And Understanding

It is said when you are young, you learn, but when you are older, you understand. Being a winner takes a level of knowledge, wisdom, and understanding. These three concepts are so different, however, very intimately connected. Knowledge is defined as the "awareness or familiarity gained by experience of a fact or situation." It is a fact, that a tomato is a fruit. Scientifically speaking, "a tomato is definitely a fruit. True fruits are developed from the ovary in the base of the flower and contain the seeds of the plant (though cultivated forms may be seedless)." Knowing this, we would never put a tomato in a fruit salad because wisdom tells us not to do so. Wisdom is the practical application of knowledge. You can have knowledge but lack wisdom. Understanding takes things to a whole different level, because with understanding you have more in-depth cognitive insight, explanation, or motivation. To be a winner, one must have clarity around knowledge, wisdom, and understanding, and how they impact the ten principles of being a winner.

Lyndon Johnson once said, "Yesterday is not ours to recover, but tomorrow is ours to win or lose." We are faced with decisions to make. These decisions, though small, are very critical in the grand weave of the fabric of being a winner. Life is made up of a series of choices. These decisions create the path to either putting us on the favorable side of winning or not. Winning is rooted in action. Please don't forget that, and because winning is action-oriented, we are responsible for each decision taken, whether it is good or bad.

> Lyndon Johnson once said, "Yesterday is not ours to recover, but tomorrow is ours to win or lose."

As we examine these ten principles of winning, please consider your own experiences and how you can gain insight, encouragement, and direction. We all want to win, but are we willing to do the things necessary to position ourselves for victory. A desire without work is only wishful thinking, and being full of wishes gets us nowhere.

Three Possible Outcomes

When it comes to outcomes, there are three possibilities: you are either winning, losing, or quitting. All three are very different concepts. Quitting turns losing into a permanent failure. Losing on the other hand, without stopping, keeps the possibility of victory alive. Winning is different because it defeats both losing and quitting. You can't win if you quit. If you are winning, you aren't losing. As we study the laws of winning, consider a time when you wanted to quit but didn't. What did you learn in the process? Was success much closer than you realized?

While going through each law, you will find ten guiding questions to help you consider things not thought about, to provoke your thinking, and perhaps push you past your comfort zone. Physical muscle growth comes as a result of the agitation of muscles, so it is with the growth of our mental faculties. As you read this book, we challenge you to expand your thinking by embracing a growth mindset. Wrestle with each question with honesty and authenticity. Doing so will deepen the impression of everything you learn through this reading. It is our intended desire that by the end of your reading you will be stronger and well on your way to winning.

"Cherish your visions and your dreams, as they are the children of your soul – the blueprint of your ultimate achievements."

NAPOLEON HILL
RENOWNED AMERICAN SELF-HELP AUTHOR

CHAPTER ONE

You Win By Having An Intended Outcome

K nowing your intended outcome is vital to becoming a winner. When we begin with the end in mind, we position ourselves toward success rather than away from it. Can you imagine playing a game and not knowing how to win, or better yet, imagine taking a road trip and not having an intended outcome or destination? Outcomes create a sense of purpose and allow our skills to be displayed and strengthened. The taste of sweet success is appealing and usually motivates us to replicate our actions in hopes of a winning streak. No one rarely, if ever, runs away from winning. Therefore, your intended outcome is absolutely critical to the success of everything you do. Let's take losing weight for example. If the outcome is to drop twenty pounds by Christmas, an appropriate diet and exercise regimen must follow suit. If not, the likelihood of success is compromised tremendously. Results are driven by effort and input. Without clear intended outcomes, one's efforts are marginalized, unfocused, and lack purpose.

Seeing Is Believing

Robert W. Taylor introduced the idea of backward design in 1949 when referring to a statement of objectives. This concept is rooted in intentional design. Intentional design is the process in which the interactions with a product, service, or business are considered at each point of the design process. Intentionality takes vision, effort, and a relentless desire to be purposeful at every step in the process. When we are grounded based on our true intentions, we operate from a position of purpose. Impulsivity is minimalized and clarity is maximized. As clarity is maximized so will productivity, because the clearer we are, the better we perform.

Having an intended outcome pushes the imagination to see the future, thus allowing you to visualize the success of your goals. When we activate our imagination to see the intended outcome, we position ourselves for an exciting ride. Napoleon Hill once said, "Whatever the mind of man can conceive and believe, it can achieve." The mind is a powerful thing and the ability to visualize is perhaps one of the most valuable faculties possessed by mankind. Consider your mental pictures. What images do you see, envision, or imagine when you think about winning? This is a critical question because our internal mental pictures impact our perspective of external factors. Most successful leaders are visionaries, meaning they have the ability to visualize and imagine an ideal future before it becomes reality. On the contrary, unsuccessful people often have visualizations clouded with fear and failure. They see themselves not reaching their goals and then their mental pictures become stifling rather than liberating. We all have imaginations; however, we must be mindful that the mental pictures we feed ourselves are imperative to our success. So, take control of your ability to visualize your successful future by feeding yourself positive and exciting mental pictures.

True North

Consider the intended outcome as the blueprint of a building. Blueprints are an abstract representation of a concrete reality. It is impressive to see a building, area, or project materialize from a simple plan on paper to a completed work. The imagination is vitally essential to the intended outcome because it serves as an abstract framework for our intended goals.

Knowing where one is headed helps to provide a true north. Your true north is a vision of your ideal condition, position, or circumstance. Many people are not clear on this point. Knowing your true north is critical because the absence of such can produce wasted time. Whatever we give our attention to creates a desire. Your true north will always point you in the direction of your intended outcome.

Consider the intended outcome as a goal. Without clear intended outcomes, life can be filled with impulsivity. Goals focus our energy. They have the power to propel us toward the desired result. When these intended outcomes are written down, we do better by them. In her 2015 study, psychologist Gail Matthews cited when people wrote their goals down; they were 42% more successful in achieving them than those who formulated outcomes in their heads. There is something worth noting about the power of writing your intended outcomes down. When we write our goals down, it is an external representation of our internal desire. Writing goals down takes the abstract and makes it more concrete. It's no secret that accomplishing goals boosts our self-esteem. The more we achieve our intended outcomes the more confident we become. Goals then become compelling in nature.

The Encoding Process

It is often said that the fading ink is more powerful than the strongest memory. According to best-selling author, Mary Morrison, the first step in reaching our intended outcome is to write your goals down. Writing down our goals helps with the encoding process. The encoding process is a biological process in the brain in which the things we perceive travel to our brain where they are analyzed, and from there decisions are made on what gets stored or what gets discarded. In layman's terms, when we think of the brain, we know that there are two hemispheres, the left and the right. The right hemisphere, or right side of the brain is where we deal with our imagination. Think of that side as the dreaming side. On the other hand, the left side of the brain is where we deal with the literal or practical things. The actualization of the imagination is produced from the left side of the brain. In other words, the right side dreams it up, but the left side makes it happen. Thus, it is critical for us to have a whole brain approach when we engage the goal setting process. Writing down our goals connects both sides of the brain and helps to send the encoding message from our brains down our spines and throughout our bodies, helping to make that goal live out in our actions. Through the process of encoding, writing our goals down literally takes our goals from imagination to reality.

Goals Produce Clarity

Written goals produce a sense of clarity. The more specific we are about our intended outcome, the clearer we will become with actualizing our goals. Specification is the key in this area. Let's take searching on Google, for example. When was the last time you searched for something on Google and noticed that your search was too broad or too vague? To illustrate this point, we looked up the word "hotels" and received over 9 billion results. We then searched for "hotels in America" and got just over 1 billion random results. To get a more specific answer, we had to search for the "number of hotels in America," which resulted in 54,200 hotels. From there, we narrowed our search to "hotels in Tampa, Florida," which produced a selection of 187 hotels. Finally, we wanted to narrow our search to a more specific brand, so we looked for Marriott hotels in downtown Tampa. The result was narrowed and focused. We got back 14 hotels in which we were able to pick one we liked.

The more specific we are, the quicker we become at narrowing our efforts and concentration. If you want a better job, you must know what better looks like. If you want a better season, you must be clear on what that season should look like. If you want a better home, you must know what things you want to put in the house to improve the quality of living you are expecting to have. Wanting better equates to knowing what better is. Failure to know what better looks like is an inability to be clear. Clarity increases productivity in all facets and increases the likelihood of reaching your intended outcome.

How To Score

Bill Copeland once said, "The trouble with not having a goal is that you can spend your life running up and down the field and never score." Goals help you score. There is a reason why basketball, hockey, and soccer players aim for goals during game time. The goal becomes the driving force of the game. Without goals, purpose is stripped. As it is with sports, the team who accomplishes the most goals wins. Knowing what you are aiming for is equally, if not more important than the skills you possess. There is greatness in all of us; however, what begins to separate the good from the great are those who are clear about their intended outcomes. Many people with exceptional talent often don't step into their full potential, simply because they lack a clear understanding of their goals and the necessary steps to achieving them.

> The more specific we are, the quicker we become at narrowing our efforts and concentration.

Here's one thing to keep in mind. If you are in a position of influence or leadership, you must help others develop or discover their intended outcome. Steven Covey, in the *Seven Habits of Highly Effective People*, discovered that effective people begin with the end in mind. It is a habit that produces winners in leadership, sports, entrepreneurship, personal productivity, and business. Coaches are always encouraging athletes to imagine successful results before competing. Knowing what victory looks like makes it easier to plan effectively and efficiently. Doing so will allow you to be able to communicate the details more readily. Furthermore, having a clear intended outcome will give the proper motivation to tackle the tasks ahead.

Greatness By Design

Clearly articulated and designed goals leave very little to chance. It allows for more intentionality with what we do, who we become, and how we manage our efforts and energy. According to Steven Covey, "If you don't make a conscious effort to visualize who you are and what you want in life, then you empower other people and circumstances to shape you and your life by default. It's about connecting again with your own uniqueness and then defining the personal, moral, and ethical guidelines within which you can most happily express and fulfill yourself." The clearer we are with who we are, what we want, and how we want it, the more we can focus on the task of accomplishing the goals set before us.

Here are a few questions to help you bring clarity to your intended outcome:

- Explain your intended outcome for one of your current goals.
- What motivates you in life?
- What obstacles are preventing or hindering you from accomplishing your intended outcome?
- Have you developed a habit of writing your goals down?
- What do you visualize when you picture your success?
- What types of mental pictures fill your head when you think about your goals? Are they positive or negative?
- What is your true north?
- How do you approach goal setting with intentionality?
- When it comes to winning, do you know your intended outcomes?
- If you are in a leadership position, how do you help others discover or develop their intended outcomes?

Do Now Exercise

Pause for a moment and think about one major goal you've set for yourself. What mental pictures come to mind when you visualize this goal? Now, write down your goal. Next, make a list of all steps and actions needed to achieve your goal. Lastly, think about when you would like to accomplish your goal, and assign a victory date.

Chapter Review

- Winners know their intended outcomes. When we begin with the end in mind, we position ourselves toward success rather than away from it.

- When we are grounded based on our true intentions, we operate from a position of purpose. Impulsivity is minimalized, and clarity is maximized. As clarity is maximized so will productivity, because the clearer we are, the better we perform.

- Having an intended outcome pushes the imagination to see the future, thus allowing you to visualize the success of your goals.

- Our internal mental pictures impact our perspective on external factors.

- Most successful leaders are visionaries, meaning they have the ability to visualize and imagine an ideal future before it becomes a reality.

- When we write our goals down, it is an external representation of our internal desire.

- Writing goals down takes the abstract and makes it more concrete.

- Knowing where one is headed helps to provide a true north. Your true north is a vision of your ideal condition, position, or circumstance.

- Many people with exceptional talent often don't step into their full potential simply because they lack a clear understanding of their goals and the necessary steps to achieving them.

- The clearer we are with who we are, what we want, and how we want it, the more we can focus on the task of accomplishing the goals set before us.

"Planning is bringing the future into the present so that you can do something about it now."

– ALLEN LAKEIN

CHAPTER TWO

You Win By Having a Game Plan

n her book *Teaching A Stone To Talk,* Annie Dillard reveals a sad but poignant story about what happens when we set out unprepared. She tells of a British Arctic expedition that set sail in 1845 to chart the Northwest Passage around the Canadian Arctic to the Pacific Ocean. Neither of the two ships and none of the 138 men aboard returned.

Captain Sir John Franklin prepared as if they were embarking on a pleasure cruise rather than an arduous and grueling journey through one of the earth's most hostile environments. He packed a 1,200-volume library, a hand-organ, china place settings for officers and men, cut-glass wine goblets and sterling silver flatware, beautifully and intricately designed. Years later, some of these place settings would be found near a clump of frozen, cannibalized bodies.

The voyage was doomed when the ships sailed into frigid waters and became trapped in ice. First, ice coated the decks, the spars, and the rigging. Then water froze around the rudders and the ships became hopelessly locked in the now-frozen sea. Sailors set out to search for help, but soon succumbed to severe Arctic weather and died of exposure to its harsh winds and sub-freezing temperatures. For some twenty years, the remains of the expedition were found all over the frozen landscape.

The crew did not prepare for the cold nor for the possibility of the ships becoming ice-locked. On a voyage that would last two to three years, they packed only their Navy-issued uniforms, and the captain carried just a 12-day supply of coal for the auxiliary steam engines. The frozen body of an officer was eventually found, miles from the vessel, wearing his uniform of fine blue cloth, edged with silk braid, a blue greatcoat and a silk handkerchief — clothing which was noble and respectful, but ultimately inadequate.

Planning Is Proactive

Most victories are won before a game begins, a war is fought, a deal is made, a test is taken, or a relationship starts. It merely begins by having a game plan. It is impressive to see the degree of game planning that takes place within the collegiate and professional sports arena to be ready for game day. Hours of films are studied. Offensive and defensive schemes are drawn up to ensure each team has a battle plan before going into action. Can you imagine going to war without a plan of attack, or without a clear strategy? Death and defeat would be the eminent result.

In the business world, the notion of a game plan is taken seriously. Before any business or corporation makes a financial investment, there must be targeted intentionality and a fail-proof game plan that will govern each step and protect the financial integrity of the investment. Game planning for the business world involves studying the community, predicting anticipated barriers, analyzing growth projection, forecasting risks, and building for the future. Having a game plan means you take a proactive approach to winning. It also means having a vision of the intended outcome.

Planning is truly one of the most proactive moves you can make. You don't blame anyone, but you take actions into your own hands. When you plan, you recognize that there is a responsibility you must fulfill. You choose not to be reactive and wait for "chance" to take you wherever the wind blows. Proactivity is rooted in planning and it is a habit of people who win. When we plan, we reason from cause to affect. We recognize consequences and seek the optimal outcome by strategizing. Planning minimizes impulsivity and increases targeted energy. Planning gives the mind a mental model before the concrete reality. Imagine a plan being like a GPS that is guiding you to a destination. It helps you to know when you are on the right track or if you are getting off the path. Plans are rooted in decision making. If you think about it, plans are a collective series of decisions strung together. At the heart of any outcome, you will find that decisions were made based on some form of planning. The better we become with our decision making the better we will be at winning.

The Power Of Planning

Planning controls impulsivity. It allows for the opportunity to remain calm under stressful situations because there is a game plan to follow. "Leaving the game plan is a sign of panic," said Chuck Noll, "and panic is not in our game plan." Planning is not the end-all, nor is it intended to remove all troubles, but it sure does decrease anxiety in so many ways. When

> Having a game plan means you take a proactive approach to winning.

anxiety is decreased, performance is enhanced which lends toward a winning disposition.

Planning is simply the beginning principle on the road to victory. Dick Vitale once said, "Coaching to me is the ultimate high, especially when you have a game plan, and you see that game plan executed to perfection. To see those players take what you put in front of them in preparation and turn it into a masterpiece – it doesn't get any better than that." That masterpiece comes truly from having a solid game plan.

At the start of every year, we have a vision retreat where we escape for a weekend to plan goals for every facet of our lives. We prepare for the following areas: spiritual, financial, health, professional, recreational, relational, marital, and parental goals. This level of planning has served us very well, and over the years has set us up for much success. The amazing thing is that we get to monitor the progress of our plans. Without a plan, there is nothing to gauge and nothing to assess to see if you are on the right track. Plans are like roadmaps, with indicators that help govern where to go and what to anticipate.

As former high school teachers, we can remember making lesson plans for the week. Although adjustments were made to those plans, they provided a framework to operate within. As a result, our weekly lesson plans afforded us the luxury of not walking into class blind or unprepared. The plan was a clear guide and often served as a mechanism for controlling several variables within the classroom. Planning prepares the way for winning.

Planning also paves the way for clear expectations. Plans drive expectations, and expectations create the standards for operation. Every winning entity has evident standards when it comes to the way they operate. But those standards of operation did not fall from the sky. They were the labor of clear planning.

Benjamin Franklin is credited with the famous quote, "failing to plan is planning to fail." We must understand that planning outlines our priorities. We can remember when we got engaged. The date was December 24th, and we were both very excited. We landed on June 24th as the wedding date and very shortly after that, all actions, efforts, talents, money, and energy were committed to planning for our special day. With so many details to consider, some people even hire a wedding planner to help them through the process of planning. Whichever route taken; the intended outcome is to simply win on the wedding day.

Short, Medium, and Long

As ambitious as you are, some goals require much more time and effort than others. While the desire for more immediate satisfaction is there, big life-changing goals usually require a game plan comprised of several mini-steps along the way. Understanding the short, medium, and long-term process of game planning is very critical when it comes to winning. Not all victories are won in four quarters. And depending on the intended outcome, your goals may require months or years of hard work and determination to come out on the winning side.

Short-term goals are your daily driver – the vehicle might not excite you, but it carries you regularly. Such goals describe the daily, weekly, or monthly actions you undertake in order to reach medium- and long-term goals. For example, let's say the long-term goal is to save $10,000 within two years. The short-term goal would be to do a weekly budget to determine your saving and spending capacity. When setting goals, each short-term goal should be a single action, prioritized for the designated time period, and should be aligned with the medium- and long-term goals.

Medium-term goals bridge the gap between short-term goals and fuel the long-term vision you have for your future. These goals serve as checkpoints along the way to meeting your long-term, big goal. The timeline for medium-term goals can range, as they are dependent on the total scope of the final intended outcome. For example, startups and newer companies typically have medium term goals lasting anywhere from one to five years. On the contrary, more viable companies that have existed longer typically have med-term goals for much longer time spans. The key to remember here is that context matters when setting goals. The goals of a novice are expected to look drastically different from those of an expert.

Lastly, long- term goals tend to be loftier than short and medium goals and are typically aligned to your compelling why or overarching purpose in life. Reaching your long-term goals may serve as a final destination or may point towards the creation of new goals.

Smarter Not Harder

When setting goals, you should always keep them SMART. According to Peter Drucker, author of Management by Objectives and developer of the SMART goal process, the acronym stands for Simple, Measurable, Achievable, Relevant, and Time-Sensitive.

Simple: Your goal should be clear and specific in order to focus your efforts and fuel your motivation. Use the five "W" test when establishing your goals to ensure that they are simple, clear, and specific.

- **What** do I want to accomplish?
- **Why** is this goal important?
- **Who** is involved?
- **Where** is it located?
- **Which** resources or limits are involved?

Measurable: Effective game planning always includes quantifiable checkpoints to measure progress along the way. Assessing progress helps you to stay focused, meet your deadlines, and conjures up excitement. A measurable goal should address questions such as:

- How much?
- How many?
- How often?
- How will I know when it is accomplished?

Achievable: While your goals may stretch your skillset and may require you to learn new things, they should also be realistic and attainable. When determining if your goals are achievable, ask yourself the following questions: An achievable goal will usually answer questions such as:

- How can I accomplish this goal?
- How realistic is the goal, based on other constraints and factors?
- Does this goal align with other goals I've set for myself?
- Will this goal get me closer to my overarching long-term goal?

Relevant: This step is about ensuring that your goals matter to you and speak towards your purpose. Along with your goals being achievable, they should also align with other relevant goals. Relevancy communicates purpose and importance. So, make sure that your plans are relevant by answering yes to the following questions:

- Is your goal worthwhile?
- Is it the right timing to tackle this goal?
- Does this goal match other efforts, needs, or priorities?
- Am I the right person to reach this goal? Or do I have the appropriate resources to assist with reaching this goal?

Time-bound: Another element of effective goal setting is applying target dates to associated tasks as well as a deadline for long-term goals. Time-bound goals provide tangible deadlines to focus on and give something to work toward. This part of the SMART goal criteria helps to prevent everyday tasks from taking priority over your longer-term goals. A time-bound goal will usually answer these questions:

- When?
- What can I do six months from now?
- What can I do six weeks from now?
- What can I do today?
- When can I achieve my long-term goal and is the timing realistic?

Here are a few questions about planning that will help you with your personal and professional life:

- Are you clear about your life's vision and mission?
- Do you know your intended outcomes?
- What is your 3 to 5-year plan?
- Can you summarize that plan with 60 seconds?
- What excites you most when you get up in the morning?
- What are some anticipated barriers you will face in reaching your intended outcomes?
- How will you celebrate your small victories?
- How will you address difficult situations?
- What area of the plan do you feel the least competent in?
- What deadlines do you need to have in place to monitor your progress?
- Who will you select as an accountability partner?
- Who do you need to talk with to gain insights and understanding?

Do Now Exercise

Now that you have written your goals down use the information shared in this chapter to make your goals SMART. After writing your SMART goals, put them somewhere visible where you can revisit them regularly.

Chapter Review

- Most victories are won before a game begins, a war is fought, a deal is made, a test is taken, or a relationship begins. It starts simply by having a game plan.

- When you plan, you recognize that there is a responsibility you must fulfill. You choose not to be reactive and wait for "chance" to take you wherever the wind blows.

- Plans are a collective series of decisions strung together. At the heart of any outcome you will find that decisions were made based on some form of planning.

- Without a plan, there is nothing to gauge and nothing to assess to see if you are on the right track.

- Plans are like roadmaps, with indicators that help govern where to go and what to anticipate.

- Planning also paves the way for clear expectations. Plans drive expectations and expectations create the standards for operation.

- Not all victories are won in four quarters. Depending on the intended outcome, your goals may require months or years of hard work and determination in order to come out on the winning side.

- Short-term goals describe the daily, weekly, or monthly actions you undertake in order to reach medium- and long-term goals.

- Medium-term goals bridge the gap between short-term goals and fuel the long-term vision you have for your future. These goals serve as checkpoints along the way to meeting your long-term, big goals.

- Long-term goals may serve as a final destination or may point toward the creation of new goals.

- When setting goals, you should always keep them SMART – Simple, Measurable, Achievable, Relevant and Time-Sensitive.

"An ounce of practice is worth more than tons of preaching."

– MAHATMA GANDHI
NON-VIOLENT ACTIVIST

CHAPTER THREE

You Win By Practicing

M uhammad Ali, one of the greatest boxers in the world said, "I hated every minute of training, but I said, 'Don't quit. Suffer now and live the rest of your life as a champion.'" Practicing is fundamental to winning. Creating muscle memory through practicing is critical for success. In a special interview with Michael Jordan for his 50th birthday, it was amazing how he answered questions about practicing. He stated that he took every practice as if it was the real game, so that when he got in the real game it was nothing more than practice. The bottom line is that he never took practice lightly and he knew the importance it played in the grand picture of winning.

Practicing takes the guessing out of situations. It creates the routines necessary for one to be successful. Professional athletes understand the importance of practicing. They run the same drills over and over until they are perfect. It has been said, don't practice until you get it right, practice until you can't get it wrong. Practice engraves the idea, concept, movement, words, or posture so well in the subconscious that it can be reproduced immediately. Practice produces muscle memory. According to Nerd Fitness, "Your muscles don't actually have brains, but rather your brains have learned to quickly call upon these quick procedure lists to get certain tasks done as quickly and efficiently as possible. The more often you complete these tasks, the less "processing power" your brain needs to complete the task and the more automatic it becomes." Muscle memory become the building blocks of better and more efficient results.

Wrong Versus Right

Conversely, practicing wrong can be detrimental to winning. Michael Jordan once said, "You can practice shooting eight hours a day, but if your technique is wrong, then all you become is very good at shooting the wrong way." Practice perpetuates the behavior so it's important that your practice is correct or else you could learn how to permanently do it wrong. That's why proper practice prevents poor performance. Practicing the right way will help to set the conditions for winning.

For one to win, practice has to be one of the legs the chair stands on. There is a reason why every successful school, company, or organization has embedded certain things that they practice routinely. Intended behaviors do not happen by chance, luck, or well wishing. It happens by the hard work of practicing.

We are reminded of a school where it was the norm for the fire drills to be noisy and rambunctious. They were accustomed to this kind of experience and it was evident that some changes needed to be made for them to be more efficient and successful in this area. The first thing we did was establish the intended outcome, which was that all students would evacuate the building silently, walking in a straight line. The irony of this situation was that many faculty and staff didn't believe in the intended outcome that the entire school could evacuate the building in this manner.

We can remember the first time we did it. We set the expectations and intended outcomes by verbally sharing them via the intercom for the entire school. From that day, until now, it has been one of the most beautiful sights to see. The more we practiced, the better we became and the better we became the more efficient we were. Practice makes things better. The purpose of practice is not to make things worse, it's to ensure improvements.

Do you practice to defeat the moment? What is your moment? We all have them. We all have these things we need to conquer and being able to face them is part of the process of winning.

Sharpen Your Axe

A young man approached the foreman of a logging crew and asked for a job. "That depends," replied the foreman. "Let's see you cut this tree." The young man stepped forward, and skillfully chopped the great tree. Impressed, the foreman exclaimed, "You can start Monday." Monday, Tuesday, Wednesday, Thursday rolled by — and Thursday afternoon the foreman approached the young man and said, "You can pick up your paycheck on the way out today."

Startled, the young man replied, "I thought you paid on Friday."

"Normally we do," said the foreman. "But we're letting you go today because you've fallen behind. "Our daily cutting charts show that you've dropped from first place on Monday to last place today."

"But I'm a hard worker," the young man objected. "I arrive first, leave last, and even have worked through my coffee breaks!" The foreman, sensing the young man's integrity, thought for a minute and then asked, "Have you been sharpening your axe?"

The young man replied, "No sir, I've been working too hard to take time for that!"

Our lives are like that. We sometimes get so busy that we don't take time to "sharpen the axe." Why is

> For one to win, practice has to be one of the legs the chair stands on.

that? Could it be that we have forgotten how to stay sharp? Playing the game of life is not enough. We must take the time to sharpen our axe through practice. This vital ingredient is what separates the good from the great. Remember, the average practice till they get it right, but the expert practices until they can't get it wrong. Practice makes permanent, it deepens the impression, and sharpens the intellect. When we take practice more seriously than winning, we are tipping the scales toward consistent victories.

God is in the Details

The idiom "God is in the details" has been dated for centuries and means attention paid to small things have big rewards, or that details are super important. One person in the sports arena who embodies this idea was John Wooden. John Wooden, UCLA's basketball team coach for 27 years, was named the "Greatest Coach of the 20th Century" by ESPN and the greatest coach ever in sports by the Sporting News. John Woodens' teams have been responsible for 10 national championships in 12 years and an 88-game consecutive winning streak. Talk about a guy that understands winning. How did he do it? His methods and ways have been studied by many in every field because winning is universal. One of the major things separating Wooden from other coaches was his laser-like focus on the importance of practicing. Practice for him included the finite details all the way down to putting on your socks. Yes, your socks. Wooden knew if his players did not correctly put their socks on, they could potentially have blisters and foot problems.

Practice often happened without the ball in order to reinforce key skills. And when the ball was introduced players were well acquainted with the conceptual knowledge, procedural knowledge, and the application of the play or skill. For example, imagine shooting without the ball or imagine practicing in a manner to replicate the actual game. Wooden kept a record of every practice and filed for future reference. That way he knew what to look back at if he ever played that team again. Unlike many coaches, he repeated the details of drills until there was mastery by all. He refused to move to the more complex skills until the minute the details had the most attention. Every minute of his practice had purpose just like every minute of a real game. He positioned the basketball racks so that players could maximize every minute in practice. You could say he took practice seriously, and as a result his players took the games as equally important, if not more important.

Hotbeds

In the book *The Talent Code* by sportswriter Daniel Coyle, he describes some of the most amazing talent hotbeds around the world and how these hotbeds may not look like the most sophisticated edifices of the 21st century and are in fact some of the most rundown places in the world. For example, consider the one indoor court in the freezing cold of Russia which has produced the top 20 women players in the game of tennis. How could this be? They don't have the latest machines on exercise science or the latest labs to test the oxygen flow of their athletes, yet they produce winners.

In *The Talent Code,* Coyle explains how the compounded effects of better practice are found in the "hot spots" of concentrated talent around the world. If you practice better, you will become better. Duplication is in the practice. Winning is in the practice. Not just any practice, the slow and correct practice. Slow and correct is always better than fast and wrong.

Additionally, Coyle also points out that the talent for soccer can be found in Brazil. Brazil's futsul, soccer, is one that is very unique in nature to soccer across the world. With futsul, Brazilians are used to playing a modified form of soccer due to field size that allows for six times more touches and quicker decision making. The ball used is not as elastic and requires a more elevated skill to master. According to Coyle, "The game space limitations reward skills learned to speedy automaticity." The reality is that the way the Brazilians practice separates them from any soccer-loved nation around the world. Their practice is built into the DNA of the nation and the cultivation of talent in their country.

Practicing is at the heart of winning and those who know how to do it well see results in the outcome of victory. Have you found the "hotbeds" for your field or career path? How do individuals within these hotbeds practice? What do they do that separates them from others and are you willing to explore the same path?

Here are a few reflection questions to consider as you analyze your practice habits:

- In what areas do you want to become an expert?
- Outside of your expertise, what are you passionate about?
- How seriously do you take practice?
- What would practice look like for them?
- Which part of practice do you avoid most?
- How would or how does practice increase your performance?
- What areas of weakness have you discovered as a result of practicing?
- How often do you need to practice to maximize your outcome?
- In what areas do you need to practice more?
- Who holds you accountable when it comes to practicing?

Do Now Exercise

Refer to your SMART goals from Chapter Two. Determine any areas where you need to practice, learn more, or refine your skillset to fully accomplish your goals. Also, consider any resources required to assist you in being successful. Next, determine a plan of action to support your efforts and write it down. Lastly, identify an individual who will hold you accountable for your practice.

Chapter Review

- Practicing takes the guessing out of situations. It creates the routines necessary for one to be successful.
- Don't practice until you get it right, practice until you can't get it wrong.
- Practice is to engrave the idea, concept, movement, words, or posture so well in the subconscious that it can be reproduced immediately.
- Practice produces muscle memory.
- Practice perpetuates the behavior, so it's essential that your practice is correct or else you could learn how to do it wrong permanently.
- The average practice till they get it right, but the expert practices until they can't get it wrong.
- Practice makes permanent; it deepens the impression and sharpens the intellect.
- If you practice better, you will become better. Duplication is in the practice.
- Winning is in the practice. Not just any practice, the slow and correct practice. Slow and proper practice is always better than fast and wrong practice.

"The person interested in success has to learn to view failure as a healthy, inevitable part of the process of getting to the top."

– JOYCE BROTHERS
FORMER AMERICAN PSYCHOLOGIST,
TELEVISION PERSONALITY, AUTHOR,
AND COLUMNIST

CHAPTER FOUR

You Win By Learning From Your Failures

ailure is a part of life. As a matter of fact, it is innately tied to the process of learning, and learning is a prerequisite for winning. When we consider babies, we usually don't count the lessons of failure and how they are vital for child development and growth. The victory of learning how to walk comes from the failures of falling as a child. Our learning is in direct proportion to the quality of failure. The quality of failure is a concept that many have misunderstood in their journey. Failure has a way of teaching humility, and before we can be great at winning, we must be humbled by such valuable lessons.

Failure and Other Approaches

In addition to creating humility, failure also forces us to consider other approaches. We must be honest; we may not have all the answers or all the angles, but if we are humble enough, we will seek other vantage points and techniques. Wilma Rudolph once said, "Winning is great, sure, but if you are really going to do something in life, the secret is learning how to lose. Nobody goes undefeated all the time. If you can pick up after a crushing defeat, and go on to win again, you are going to be a champion someday." Failure helps us understand we are human and that we are not without limitations. These limitations can be enhanced, but until then, failure is here to remind us that we are not better than anyone. Skills and talents may make us better off but never better than others. This is a very critical lesson in humility.

Failure and Knowledge

Failure also causes us to grow in knowledge. When you fail, the first-hand insights are priceless because you can harness what you learn for more positive outcomes in the future. Let's consider for one moment the well-known household cleaning product, Formula 409. This product is one of the great inspirations as it relates to failure and the knowledge gained towards creating a winning recipe. "The Formula 409® name is actually a tribute to the tenacity of two young Detroit scientists hell-bent on formulating the greatest grease-cutting, dirt-destroying, bacteria cutting cleaner on the planet." Creating this amazing formula took much patience, strenuous effort, and consistent attempts. It didn't happen after the 200th, 300th or 400th attempt, it wasn't until batch 409 that the formula was finally perfected. Hence the cleaner was named Formula 409. If we need a lesson from Formula 409 it would be that a winning formula can be created through failure. And just like the developers behind Formula 409, there are countless examples of highly accomplished individuals who faced repeated failure before stepping into their success or greatness. In other words, greatness is born on the edge of failure.

Michael Jordan, arguably one of the greatest basketball players in the sport, once said "I've missed more than 9000 shots in my career. I've lost almost 300 games. 26 times, I've been trusted to take the game winning shot and missed. I've failed over and over again in my life. And that is why I succeed." Michael Jordan was not afraid to fail and because he was not afraid to fail, it gave him the courage to be a winner. We must re-envision how we view failure. We must harness its great potential and utilize it for future victories. Another relevant example of turning failure into victory is the success story of comedian Jim Carrey. Carrey grew up in a lower-income family with a father who struggled to maintain steady employment. Due to their financial struggles, Carrey eventually had to drop out of high school at the age of 15 and worked as a janitor just to help support the family. Ironically, on his first comic stand-up gig, Carrey ended up being booed off stage. Adding to that, when he later auditioned for Saturday Night Live for the 1980–81 season, he failed to land the part.

We all know about Carrey's later success, but few are aware that his early years were quite the contrast from the fame now depicted in mainstream society. In an interview with Oprah Winfrey, Carrey shared how he wrote himself a check for 10 million dollars for "Acting Services Rendered," later placing the check in his wallet for 7 years until he received a 10-million-dollar payment for his work in *Dumb And Dumber.* Oftentimes, temporary failure precedes success.

Failure and Patience

One of the greatest virtues in life is patience. Patience is the capacity to accept or tolerate delay, trouble, or suffering without getting angry or upset. Have you ever lost at something and got angry about it? Better yet, have you ever got angry and did something that you regret or could not imagine. The reason for this is that when we get angry the prefrontal cortex, the section of the brain that helps us weigh decisions, shuts down making it difficult to think rationally. At the same time the Amygdala, the threat detector of the body heightens, causing our adrenalin to increase and our fight or flight mentality to kick in. This is turn suppresses our rational thinking and memory. This explains why sometimes it is hard to remember the details of what happened during times of anger.

Failure has a way to test and to reveal our patience and our patience has a way of testing our anger. At the end of the day, patience is a choice. When we choose to be patient, we have to make a conscious decision to respond to a negative situation in a positive way. Instead of losing it, we remain under control and our fuse never reaches the bomb to explode. Anger is an emotion that could manifest itself in failure due to unmet desires or needs.

Winners never look at failure as the end of the game, they look at failure as the beginning of possibilities. Failure pushes them to slow down and analyze. It gives them an opportunity to control their emotions rather than allowing their emotions to take them all over the place. Patience is a process and failure is a great teacher of that process if we would submit to the lessons. Patience does not come naturally so failure produces opportunities to better ourselves in the arena of patience and tolerance. It is what we learn through failing moments that produces a winning character.

Failure and Character

Failure develops character. Patience is a virtue that produces other virtuous characteristics. For example, tolerance is an extension of patience. Forbearance is an extension of patience. Patience has a high yield in character development. We are reminded of moments early in our careers where we tried to advance in our field. We applied for different positions and unfortunately, we were not successful at winning. Though devastated because we didn't get our desired positions, it clearly galvanized us to work harder, prepare better, gain more experience and develop our character. It has always been our observation that when a fruit is picked before its time it is never sweet. Most of the time it is bitter and lacks the maturity and natural flavor which is innately within fruit. Many never come to realize that failures are just the result of not reaching maturity, or the fullness of time has not come yet. You see, when the fullness of time comes, that fruit will one day have a perfect moment. That moment will be when the fruit is at its very best in texture, color, flavor and smell. We can have a winning season in life when we learn how to pick those fullness of time moments, actions, events, or decisions better. Eventually the fullness of time moment did come, and we were selected for our respective positions.

Here are a few questions about failure that will help you in your personal and professional life.

- What failure in your life has brought the most humility to your experience so far?
- What has been the greatest growth opportunity so far that you have had from a failure?
- If you could pick one failure you could get a second chance, what would it be and why?
- What failure are you most ashamed of and have you dealt with the guilt of that shame?
- What failure has caused you the most resentment?
- How do you typically handle failure?
- Which failure brought you the greatest insight and what was it?
- Explain one victory you see now that came out of clear failure?
- What creative experience have you had as a result of failure?
- What's your "fullness of time failure" that needed to be matured more?

Failure has a way to test and reveal our patience and our patience has a way of testing our anger.

Do Now Exercise

Think about a time when you were not successful. How did you respond to your failure? Write down your natural tendencies when it comes to responding to failure. Next, reflect on how such responses have either grown your character or hindered it. Lastly, create a game plan for how you will respond to failure in a manner that will put you on the winning path.

Chapter Review

- Failure is a part of life. As a matter of fact, it is innately tied to the process of learning and learning is a prerequisite for winning.
- Skills and talents may make us better off but never better than others. This is a very critical lesson in humility.
- Greatness is born on the edge of failure.
- Not being afraid to fail gives us the courage to try and the desire to be a winner.
- Oftentimes, temporary failure precedes success.
- Failure has a way to test and to reveal our patience and patience has a way to test and reveal our anger.
- When we choose to be patient, we have to make a conscious decision to respond to a negative situation in a positive way.
- Patience is a virtue that produces other virtuous characteristics.
- It is what we learn through failing moments that produces a winning character.
- We can have a winning season in life when we learn how to pick those fullness of time moments, actions, events, or decisions better.

"When it is obvious that your goals cannot be reached, don't adjust the goals, adjust the actions."

– CONFUCIUS
LEGENDARY CHINESE PHILOSOPHER
AND POLITICIAN

CHAPTER FIVE

You Win By Making Game Time Adjustments

n 2017 the world witnessed one of the greatest comebacks in Superbowl history. The New England Patriots under the leadership of quarterback Tom Brady played the Atlanta Falcons for the Superbowl title that year. The Patriots found themselves in a very precarious situation being down 25 points in the fourth quarter. With such a bleak situation, the New England Patriots had to make some game time adjustments to even have a chance of coming back and winning the game. Play after play the Patriots made the right adjustments to counter the Atlanta Falcons offense and defense. Without the appropriate adjustments by the Patriots the game would have been over. Game time adjustments helped the Patriots go down in history as the winners of Super Bowl LI with the final score of 34 to 28.

Adjustments Are Necessary

Making game time adjustments is an essential part of the game of life. The most planned outcome could be altered by an unforeseen circumstance. In these moments, flexibility and responsiveness is the name of the game. Failure to make adjustments leaves us in a fixed mindset and inevitably can cause us to take a loss. Winning requires us to make game time adjustments. Think about the first sport that comes to mind. A coach has to make numerous game time decisions that can ultimately shape the outcome of the match. As a coach builds their episodic knowledge, they are able to pull from past experiences quickly to make the best call in the moment. A coach must decide which substitution is best and the appropriate time to make that call. A coach has to decide on the tempo of the game, and if things should speed up or slow down. Coaches use their time-outs carefully and wisely as a defensive or offensive strategy. Every decision is a careful adjustment to maximize the winning potential.

The Game of Life

These adjustments are very much applicable to the game of life. The first step in this equation is to recognize that there is a problem and that adjustments have to be made for a more favorable outcome. Recognizing the need for adjustment is equally as important as the adjustments themselves. Where the need can't be seen, the adjustment is often not welcomed or administered.

Think about game time adjustments as a problem-solving mindset. Top performers in every field are usually problem solvers. They know how to make adjustments to solve problems. Throughout the course of life, we will fall into countless amounts of problems: financial, family, physical, spiritual, and emotional problems to name a few. If you have problems, you are alive. Problems are like bills; they never go away and they return regularly. Problems have a way to bring the best or the worst out of us. This is why it is essential that we understand and harness effective practices during times when game time adjustments are highly needed.

Remaining calm under high stress situations is a particular skill-set that most top performers possess. When we are calm during game time adjustments it enables us to activate the "thinking brain." Fear begets fear and ultimately begins to shut down the neocortex which affects clear thinking. When problems arise will you activate your thinking brain to make the game time adjustments needed or will you fold in fear? Game time adjustments are more about reworking vs reacting. When we react, we operate from a deficit model. When we rework, we operate from a proactive framework. There are plans that we will need to rework verses react to. We will need to examine what or who needs to stay or go. We may have to rework our approach at the task or even consider if that is the task needed to win. Reworking the plan puts us back into the driver's seat and helps us take control of our circumstances. Reworking the plan means that we are back to examining the law of having a game plan. We are not beginning from ground zero but reworking the game plan so that we can arrive at the intended outcome of winning.

When was the last time you had to call a timeout in your life so that you can regroup your efforts or slow your opponent down? As mentioned earlier, game time adjustments come in many ways. Putting a temporary pause on the play, such as a timeout, is a strategy in every sport. This allows the teams to communicate and to determine offensive or defensive strategies, inspire morale, or just to catch a breath. There are times you will need to determine your game time adjustments to place yourself in a winning situation.

Going into halftime can be scary sometimes, especially if you are down by many points. In these moments, it is important that you don't overemphasize the negative so that you don't lose sight of what's working or what's going well. Is your brain like most people? Wired to examine the negative first. Seek to celebrate what's going well so that you can build on it. Remember halftimes and timeouts are not forever. They are moments in time for us to rework the plan so that the game time adjustments place us in a winning position. In the game of life, vacation time could be considered a halftime moment. Just like in a sport, vacations are halftime moments that allow for regrouping, recalibrations, and game time adjustments. We seldom view vacations in this manner because we are usually preoccupied with looking at it as a break from reality. In essence, vacations serve as opportunities to return refreshed, renewed, and refocused on the objective of winning.

Every Minute Counts

It is very fascinating to watch the details that are sometimes put into a 15-minute halftime break. For great coaches, these times are highly structured and leave no room for error or idle time. Unproductive time is an enemy to winning. Time is our most precious commodity and it is afforded to every person equally. We are all given 24 hours in a day; however, what we do with that time separates those who win from those who lose. Every minute matters in our lives. We must be careful not to waste them. For example, examine this 15-minute window of a sports team and how they utilize every minute to make game time adjustments.

Utilize every minute:

Minutes 0-2: Meet with your staff on the bench and take notes, then make your way to the locker room.

Minutes 2-3: Make general comments about the first half.

Minutes 3-8: Review the first half from an offensive and defensive standpoint while noting second-half adjustments.

Minutes 8-10: Re-emphasize the second-half changes in a succinct understandable language.

Minutes 10-14: Head back to the court/field and start second-half warm-up.

Minutes 14-15: Reiterate adjustments one final time before the second half begins.

When you step into your half-time break or your timeouts, are you focused with your time and efforts? Do you have people around you that you consider part of your coaching staff? Could they have seen things another way or could you gain insights from their perspective? There is a wise proverb from King Solomon that states, "in the abundance of counselors there is victory." Proverbs 11:14. Over your lifetime you will see many sporting events. Pay attention to the game time adjustments that the winning team makes. Have you ever seen giants fall due to the adjustments the other team made? Effort can overcome talent. Think about your opponent as a task or project you are working to accomplish. Have you maximized every minute in order to win at accomplishing the task at hand? Consider how you will make game time adjustments during every half and during every quarter.

> They are moments in time for us to rework the plan so that the game time adjustments place us in a winning position.

In addition to halftime or time outs, game time adjustments can also come in the form of changing tempos. Tempo is a vital ingredient in life and in all sports. There are times when the tempo has to be sped up and times when it must be slowed down. Tempo controls our energy output. Running a high tempo offense or defense over a long period of time can cause burnout when energy is needed most to finish the game.

The key to tempo is finding the conditions that work best for you at the time that is best for you. This is considered game time situational awareness. It is your ability to apply the right decision to the right situation at the right time.

Here are two times when you could consider speeding up the pace of tempo:

1. **When momentum is on your side.** If you are on a roll don't slow down the tempo. You may lose the edge. That's why many teams call timeout when another team starts a run. They

want to change the tempo. Seize momentum when you have it and keep moving on. Your energy will serve you well in these conditions.

2. **When opponents are dragging their feet.** You must pick up the pace. My father taught me a poem when I was a child, but I didn't understand it fully until in my college years. It was from Henry Longfellow: "The heights by great men reached and kept were not attained by sudden flight, but they while their companions slept, were toiling upward in the night." If we had to reword it for this generation it would simply mean, "when others drag their feet, you have to keep pushing the tempo."

Here are two times when you could consider slowing down the pace of tempo:

1. **When you are overmatched.** It's not the dog in the fight it's the fight in the dog. A stronger opponent may want you out of their way quickly. Keep yourself in the game much longer by slowing the tempo. Haste makes waste. Sometimes when you slow down you move ahead much faster at winning. You are able to see your opponent's weakness and are able to frustrate their efforts toward you. Sometimes it's better when you're "slow to speak and quick to listen". That's changing tempo in your life. A slower tempo can save you energy and give you clarity for victory.

2. **When you are making unforced errors, you must take a hard look at yourself and slow down your pace.** Unforced errors are often caused by a lack of focus. Discipline is the natural result of staying focused and the more focused we are, the more disciplined we become. When we slow down the tempo of our lives, we are able to focus better which naturally brings back the discipline needed to be victorious.

Substitutions Aren't All Bad

Another form of game time adjustment is substitutions. On any given team you will have your starting lineup and you're off the bench players. Successful teams have benches that are deep, talented and versatile in skillset. Coaches make substitutions to position a team for winning. A coach may run many variables within their minds to determine who gets subbed into the game. Some examples for substituting a player may include, but not limited to rest, injury, fouls, skill-set, talent, and timing. Substituting is a game-time adjustment that takes skill and complex thinking. Unfortunately, oftentimes this art is taken for granted by the untrained eye.

Your Top Five

As in sports, it is said that we all have a starting lineup. Who are the people we spend the most time with? Motivational speaker Jim Rohn has famously said that we are a division of the five people we spend the most time with. "According to research by social psychologist Dr. David McClelland of Harvard [the people you habitually associate with] determine as much as 95 percent of your success or failure in life." If this is true who comes off the bench in our lives matters. These individuals affect and shape who we are and who we will become.

Your starting five should be carefully considered. How could you actively construct your social environment? Don't leave it up to chance or wishful thinking. Negative people hold us back while positive people propel us toward our intended outcomes. If we are to win, our starting five and bench players have to be contributors to our game of life. If they don't contribute, they are taking away. Here is one thing to consider when selecting your starting five. Are they people you admire? Those people are in a position you aspire to be, and their attitudes and dispositions have a more lasting impact on who you become. So simply ask yourself, who do you spend the most time with and are they people you admire?

At times you may have to make some hard decisions on who gets the playing time in the arena of your life. There may be some draft picks that you will have to trade because the return on investment is costing you a fortune. Sometimes we pay with the most valuable resource we possess and that is our time. Knowing who is your solid five and who to substitute in your life at critical moments is key to making the game time decisions needed to win.

Here are a few questions to consider when determining the needed game time adjustments for winning:

- Identify the immediate game time adjustments required in your life?
- In what areas of your life are timeouts needed?
- How do you maximize your halftime moments when working on a project or task?
- What part of your plan needs to be reworked?
- In what areas of life do you need to speed up the tempo?
- In what areas of life do you need to slow down the tempo?
- Are you encountering any unforced errors? If so, how will you make adjustments?
- Who are your starting five?
- Identify one person who should be removed from your starting five?
- Who do you admire that is not in your starting five?

Do Now Exercise

Reflect on your game plan. Determine if any adjustments need to be made immediately and write them down. Additionally, write down your top five and how each individual positively adds value to your life. After doing so, contemplate if any adjustments need to be made to your list and how you will go about making the necessary changes.

Chapter Review

- Making game time adjustments is an essential part of the game of life because the most planned outcome could be altered by an unforeseen circumstance.
- Failure to make adjustments leaves us in a fixed mindset and inevitably can cause us to take a loss.
- Top performers in every field are usually problem solvers. They know how to make adjustments to solve problems.
- Remaining calm under high-stress situations is a particular skillset that most top performers possess. When we are calm during game time adjustments, it enables us to activate the "thinking brain."
- Game time adjustments are more about reworking vs. reacting. When we react, we operate from a deficit model; however, when we rework, we operate from a proactive framework.
- Time is our most precious commodity, and it is afforded to every person equally; therefore, unproductive time is an enemy to winning.
- Game time situational awareness is your ability to apply the right decision to the right situation at the right time.
- When we slow down the tempo of our lives we can focus better, which naturally brings back the discipline needed to be victorious.
- When you are making unforced errors, you must take a hard look at yourself and slow down your pace. Unforced errors are often caused by a lack of focus.
- We are a division of the five people we spend the most time with. Determine which individuals are within your top five.

"Every weakness contains within itself a strength."

– SHUSAKU ENDO
FAMOUS CONTEMPORARY
JAPANESE WRITER

CHAPTER SIX

You Win By Identifying and Addressing Your Weaknesses

The story is told of a 10-year-old boy who decided to study Judo even though he had lost his left arm in a devastating car accident. The boy began lessons with an old Japanese Judo Master, Sensei. The boy was doing well, so he couldn't understand why, after three months of training, the master had taught him only one move. "Sensei," the boy finally said, "Shouldn't I be learning more moves?' "This is the only move you know, and this is the only move you will need," the Sensei replied. Not quite understanding, but believing in his teacher, the boy kept training.

Several months later, the Sensei took the boy to his first tournament. Surprising himself, the boy easily won his first two matches. The third match proved to be more difficult, but after some time, his opponent became impatient and charged. The boy deftly used his one move to win the match. Still amazed by his success, the boy was now in the finals. This time, his opponent was bigger, stronger and more experienced. For a while, the boy appeared to be overmatched. Concerned that the boy might get hurt, the referee called a timeout. He was about to stop the match when the Sensei intervened. "No," the Sensei insisted, "Let him continue." Soon after the match resumed, his opponent made a critical mistake. He dropped his guard. Instantly, the boy used his move to pin him. The boy had won the match and the tournament. He was the champion.

On the way home, the boy and the Sensei reviewed every move in each and every match. Then the boy summoned the courage to ask what was really on his mind. "Sensei, how did I win the tournament with only one move?" "You won for two reasons," the Sensei answered. "First, you've almost mastered one of the most difficult throws in all of Judo. And second, the only known defense for that move is for your opponent to grab your left arm." The boy's biggest weakness had become his strength.

Honesty and Vulnerability

An essential part of winning is knowing that you have weaknesses and working hard to overcome them. No one is an expert at all things. We all have our limitations and our shortcomings; however, the essential question is, what do we do with them and how do we maximize our success despite areas where we may fall short?

When identifying your weaknesses, it is vitally important to be brutally honest with yourself. You must take into account what psychologist Howard Gardner calls intrapersonal intelligence. People who have high intrapersonal intelligence are aware of their emotions, motivations, beliefs, and goals. There are some truths about yourself that you alone are aware of. Pride then becomes the biggest struggle because we must be vulnerable enough to admit our weaknesses and need for help. Our pride has a way of tripping us and then holding us down.

The first step to overcoming personal weaknesses is based on two principles: honesty and vulnerability. Many people spend most of their time in a state of emotional dishonesty. They never come to the point of being honest with themselves. Honesty and vulnerability are what we call strength moves. They allow us to confront our weaknesses and open ourselves up for improvement. Without honesty and vulnerability, we are hardened by our lies and crippled by pride.

Internal and External Weaknesses

There are also some weaknesses that only those within your starting five may know about you. These individuals sit within your blindside and can see strengths and weaknesses outside of what you are able to see within yourself. They are able to give you critical feedback about what needs to be corrected so you can live the best version of your life. "No man is an island," said John Donne. We need others to review the film of our lives and to give us timely and honest feedback so that we can make improvements. Weaknesses are fueled by internal or external factors. Always worrying about the opinions of others is an example of an internal weakness. Arriving late to work daily is a form of an external weakness. Ironically, some internal weaknesses can manifest themselves as external weaknesses and conversely; some external weaknesses can take root as internal weaknesses. It is equally important to note that our weaknesses can sometimes become compounded if they are not addressed. Weaknesses can grow, and if not addressed appropriately can become worse and may produce deeper issues.

Identifying the Source of Your Weaknesses

Weaknesses have sources. The deeper you dig, the more clarity you will find around the weakness. Have you ever examined a weakness and asked yourself at least five questions of "why" to seek the root cause of it? Here is an example to consider from a client. This client's weakness was that they were very critical of themselves. When asked, "Why are you so critical of yourself"? The answer was, "because I am a perfectionist" Why are you a perfectionist? "I think I am a perfectionist because I like things done a certain way." Why do you like things done a certain way? The response was, "when things are done a certain way, you can predict success." Why do you like to predict success? "It helps me control the variables." Why do you like to control the variables? "I like to control the variables because I don't like to fail when the stakes are high." The final question was simply, why? "Because it affects my livelihood."

All behaviors have a purpose and it's very important that we seek to understand the purpose and source of our deficits. Coaches study film to improve their team's weaknesses and also to maximize on their opponents' shortcomings. At the end of the day, weaknesses can serve as growth opportunities.

Define Your Weakness As A Goal

A weakness is an opportunity to set a goal. After an honest and vulnerable conversation with yourself and others about your weaknesses, it's time to take action. Taking action means you will have to establish a new set of habits and ways of thinking, which will then begin to shape your actions and decision making. As we think, so are we. According to Brian Tracey, "Once you become absolutely clear about what it is you want and then discipline yourself to do more of those things that move you toward this goal, your ultimate success is virtually guaranteed."

List the area(s) you desire to see improvements. When setting a goal, it cannot be broad and unclear. Your goals must be S.M.A.R.T. and values-driven, as discussed previously in chapter two. Goals should move you toward your values. If you are unclear about your core values, then perhaps this is an area in your life where you may need clarity. What are your core values and why do you have them? Values are usually shaped by the experiences we have had in our lives. Your personal core values will define who you are. All your goals should serve to work towards your core tenants. If you don't have a set of core values this is a great time to establish them and write them down. Ask yourself these three questions: What values are essential to me? What values represent my primary ways of thinking and being? What values are essential to support the best version of me? When you know your core values you will begin to understand your brand. Your brand is what you do, how you do it, and what makes you unique. This will inevitably help set you apart from others.

In addition to value-added, your goals need to be simple, measurable, attainable, realistic, and time-oriented. For example, if you wanted to work on not being too critical of yourself, it wouldn't be wise to set a goal of being more affirming daily. This goal would be too broad, and it lacks the criteria for being a S.M.A.R.T goal. For it to be SMART it would sound more like I would like to affirm my daily efforts by recognizing and writing down two positive things I have accomplished that day before I go to bed. Is it simple: write down two positive affirmations. Is it measurable: two positive affirmations can be seen in a book. Is it Attainable: two positive things can be found in a day. Is it realistic: can it be done. Is it time-bound: before going to bed daily.

The goals you have set will then become your strategic plan for improving your weaknesses. Consider your strategic plan as a way of defining your strategies, directions, and decision making for how you allocate your resources around improving your weaknesses. The reason why this is so vital is because doing so gives a sense of direction and a clear purpose. Purpose impacts performance. This new-found strategic plan can be a guide for your day-to-day decisions and also for evaluating progress toward your goals.

> The goals you have set will then become your strategic plan for improving your weaknesses.

When analyzing your weaknesses, consider these ten reflection questions.

1. List one weakness that is currently hindering your goal(s)?
2. Aside from the weakness listed above, what other weaknesses have been shared with you by others?
3. What is the source(s) of your weakness? (Use the five why method)
4. When confronting your weaknesses do you struggle most with honesty or vulnerability?
5. Who will be your accountability partner to help with your weaknesses?
6. What are your core values?
7. Where did you get your core values from?
8. Do your weaknesses compromise any of your core values? If so, how?
9. When and how do you plan to implement your strategic plan?
10. How will you celebrate small victories?

Do Now Exercise

Commit to being honest with yourself about your weaknesses. List three weaknesses in your personal and professional life. Of the three, list them in order ranging from most impactful to least impactful on your life. Next, take each weakness and create a goal that will inevitably produce an opportunity for success. Lastly, create a SMART strategic plan for addressing each gap.

Chapter Review

- An essential part of winning is being aware of your weaknesses and working hard to overcome them.
- When identifying your weaknesses, it is vitally important to be brutally honest with yourself.
- The first step to overcoming personal weaknesses is based on two principles: honesty and vulnerability. Many people spend most of their time in a state of emotional dishonesty and never come to the point of being completely honest with themselves.
- Some weaknesses can only be identified by those within your starting five. These individuals sit within your blindside and can give you critical feedback about what needs to be corrected so you can live the best version of your life.
- Our weaknesses can sometimes become compounded if they are not addressed. Weaknesses can grow, and if not addressed appropriately can become worse and may produce deeper issues.
- All behaviors have a purpose, and it's very important that we seek to understand the purpose and source of our deficits.
- A weakness is an opportunity to set a goal.
- Taking action means you will have to establish a new set of habits and ways of thinking, which will then begin to shape your actions and decision making.
- Goals should move you toward your values. If you are unclear about your core values, then this is an area in your life you need clarity.
- Your strategic plan is a method for determining how you will allocate your resources around improving your weaknesses. This is vital because it gives a sense of direction and clear purpose. Purpose impacts performance.

"Yesterday's home runs don't win today's games."

-BABE RUTH
FORMER AMERICAN BASEBALL PLAYER

CHAPTER SEVEN

You Win By Knowing Your Opponents

n competitive sports, studying game tape of the opponent can reveal a lot about their strengths, weaknesses, strategies, and favorite plays. Knowing the competitive capacity of your opponent is critical in the art of war and is often a determining factor in knowing how to make game-time adjustments. Although competition is being used as an analogy here, this same principle is applicable to the notion of winning in life.

Sun Tzu, the author of *The Art Of War*, was a master in ancient Chinese military strategies and tactics, which were not only essential for warfare but in the business world as well. According to Tzu, "If you know the enemy and know yourself, you need not fear the result of a hundred battles. If you know yourself but not the enemy, for every victory gained you will also suffer a defeat. If you know neither the enemy nor yourself, you will succumb in every battle." Tzu's original intent centered around principals of winning in war; however, oppositions put before us in life come in many different packages. These stumbling blocks may come by way of marital problems, financial strongholds, addictions, or workplace adversity just to name a few. Your strategic plan is a way of defining your strategies, directions, and making decisions on the way you will allocate your resources around improving your weaknesses. The reason why this is so vital is that it gives a sense of direction and a clear purpose. Purpose impacts performance. When it comes to winning in life, it is imperative to identify factors that are stifling your growth and then dig deep in order to get to the root causes. It is also essential to understand your role, if any, in contributing to the issues at play in your life.

As discussed in the previous chapter, you win by knowing your weaknesses, and once those weaknesses have been identified, you become empowered to strategize effectively against whatever odds are against you. The key to winning in life means removing the blinders that often create a tunnel-vision perspective. One must think "big picture" and must be open to considering the impact external factors play toward their ultimate success. While you may not be able to control such factors, studying the gamebook of those elements is essential. In essence, you want to play to the weaknesses of your opposition. For example, if you are looking to improve your marriage, it would

> Winning is about being able to identify and mitigate all distractions hindering growth, progress, and success.

be critical to identify the weaknesses in your relationship, the root causes of those issues, and then strategize in a manner to improve based on the identified struggles within your marriage. Oftentimes individuals create their roadmaps based on what they do well without taking time to strategize against the oppositional factors impeding their growth. While we know winning is about doing something exceptionally well over a continual period of time, it is just as important to remember that winning is also about focusing on what we don't do so well and making the necessary changes to improve. In essence, having a high degree of self-awareness is crucial in understanding how to maneuver through oppositional circumstances.

Understanding Opposition

When we speak of oppositional circumstances, this is not merely deduced to competitive sports or dealing with difficult people we encounter in life. Albeit, the title of this chapter may be a little limiting at first glance; however, when we consider the magnitude of life, opposition is so much more than overcoming struggles with arduous individuals or taking the victory lap after a long-sought out competition. To clarify, opposition is defined by Webster's dictionary as "the inclination to resist." Furthermore, Webster provides the following synonyms for the word oppose: "combat, resist, withstand, to set oneself against someone or something. Opposition can apply to any conflict, from mere objection to bitter hostility or warfare." Eliyahu Goldratt discusses the "theory of constraints" in his book The Goal. According to this theory, there are always constraints, or limiting factors, between you and your accomplishments. And these factors often determine your probability of success. As discussed previously, winning involves identifying your internal and external weaknesses.

Winning is about being able to identify and mitigate all distractions hindering growth, progress, and success. The world is full of distractions. We are now, more than ever, inundated with unbounded interruptions that intrude on our time and space - emails, text messages, social media alerts, cell phone calls, and a host of apps. According to *Overload!: How Too Much Information Is Hazardous To Your Organization,* unnecessary interruptions cost the U.S. economy $997 billion in 2010. And with a decade of new technologies, that figure as increased tremendously. In addition to that, chronic and unexpected disruptions in life reduce attention spans, drive stress by burning up mental and emotional resources, and trigger mistakes. One study measured the effects of forced interruptions on resident surgeons performing gallbladder removal surgeries found that surgical mistakes occurred 44 percent of the time when surgeons were distracted while only about six percent of errors occurred when no distractions were present. According to this study, interruptive questions triggered the most errors, followed by sidebar conversations.

These intruders have become nearly impossible to avoid; however, with the right amount of focus and determination, many of our distractions can be reduced or eliminated. We must also understand that entertaining distractions can be costly, and if entertained repeatedly over time, can rob us of fulfilling our appointed purpose in life. So, ask yourself, what distractions are currently serving as oppositional forces to your winning path in life.

Dealing With Difficult People

Life is one big relationship. Relationships are key and are often the "make" or "break" factor in most success stories. Possessing healthy interpersonal and relational skills are such huge components to winning. While some have a natural talent for interpersonal skills and implicitly understand what's needed to get along with others, others have to work intentionally in this particular area of their life. When dealing with difficult people, one's natural inclination might be to avoid the person out of fear of not wanting to disrupt the flow of things. However, winners don't win by avoiding difficult situations or people. Instead, they study their opponents and then strategize. Essentially, the art of dealing with difficult people is all about your own ability to respond effectively. It is more so about you, rather than the outside individual and requires a great deal of looking inward. Successful individuals can analyze their response approaches and then make the necessary adjustments. This approach takes self-awareness and humility, which builds character. It is said that one's character cannot be developed in the absence of difficult people. They are needed to make us better.

Difficult people often bring about having to engage in difficult conversations. The degree of your success in reaching your goals is highly parallel to your ability to have difficult conversations appropriately and when necessary. According to Susan Scott, author of *Fierce Conversations*, the conversation is the relationship, and we must come from behind the conversation in order for true transformation to occur. Real change during hard situations requires interrogating reality, rather than avoiding it. When it comes to dealing with difficult people, successful individuals are aware of when and how to go about having tough talks with others, while mitigating as much stress as possible.

Responding ineffectively to difficult people or situations can be costly, not only to your success but also to your health. Studies show that stress can have a lasting, negative impact on the brain. For example, a few days of stress compromises the neurons in the hippocampus, an important brain area responsible for reasoning and memory. Furthermore, weeks of unmanaged stress can cause reversible damage to neuronal dendrites (the small "arms" that brain cells use to communicate with each other), and months of stress can permanently destroy neurons. When stress is out of control, your brain and performance suffer and can ultimately impact your interpersonal interactions with others. When anxiety goes up, inappropriate behavior is the natural result. Think about the last time you acted out of character. You will likely find that during out of character moments, your stress levels are elevated, and anxiety has gotten the best of you.

Here are six key questions to ask yourself when analyzing how well you respond to difficult individuals:

1. What emotional tornadoes are created by the difficult people in your life?
2. How do difficult people react to your reactions?
3. Are you growing unhealthy actions and reactions in response to difficult people?
4. Are you the difficult person driving others to reactive behaviors?
5. How do others react to your actions and responses?
6. How do you react to difficult people in your life?

It is evident that dealing with difficult people can have compounded implications. When it comes to winning with people, consider implementing these approaches and principles on a regular basis:

- **Understand the "expectation shift,"** which occurs when the best interest and potential of an individual outweighs the preconceived biases and past experiences of a person. This perspective allows us to see others through the lens of their potential, rather than focus on their deficits. When dealing with difficult people, this is especially important because it helps to self-regulate our emotions and limits impulsive reactions.
- **Use the lens of realistic optimism.** This lens requires you to consider the actual facts of a situation, while also challenging your own confirmation biases. Using this lens requires asking yourself three simple questions: What are the facts in this situation? What's the story I'm telling myself about those facts? What do I really want as an outcome?
- **Use the reverse lens.** This lens requires empathy by viewing situations through the lens of the person who triggered you. It allows you to intellectually identify with the person even if you haven't experienced the situation personally. It doesn't mean sacrificing your own point of view but rather widening your perspective.

With the reverse lens, you ask yourself: What is this person feeling, and in what ways does that make sense? Where's my responsibility in all this?

- **Leverage your self-control.** Know yourself. Having a clear sense of self, what causes you tension, and where your limits are can serve you well when interacting with people that you find to be difficult. Staying calm and developing your emotional intelligence skills can help you to manage your reactions to frustrating situations.

- **During difficult situations, seek to understand and gain clarity by asking questions.** When clarity is heightened, inappropriate behavior and stress is reduced.

- **Don't live on an island.** Seek the advice of others. Remember that you are not the only person who has ever had to productively interact with a difficult person. Seeking out the advice of others or finding someone to help coach you through difficulties can be quite beneficial. Sometimes, talking it out can help you reframe the situation to a place where you can facilitate a more positive outcome.

Boundaries

In addition to the above strategies, one of the best approaches to dealing with difficult people is setting clear boundaries. Boundaries communicate expectations and ward off unexpected disruptions. In a physical sense, boundaries are easy to see. They come in the form of fences, signs, and manicured lawns with hedges. They communicate where one area stops and where another begins. They also communicate what is permissible and what isn't. The same is true when it comes to creating boundaries in our life. Although not as easy to see, our boundaries communicate to others who we are and who we are not. Our boundaries define us and set the tone for our expectations. When expectations are clearly communicated by way of our behavior and decision making, the likelihood of having difficulties with others is minimized significantly.

Eliminating Distractions

Establishing reasonable and realistic boundaries is necessary in order to keep interruptions and distractions at bay. Life is anarchy without boundaries, like a city would be without traffic lights. Consider the list of strategies below if you are looking for practical ways to reduce or eliminate unexpected intrusions in your life.

- Establish daily "no interruption" timeframes. During these time periods, refrain from all disruptive behaviors (checking email, clicking on ads, text messaging, and social media just to name a few).
- Use the auto-reply feature on email to communicate that you are unable to respond within the designated "no interruption" time period.
- During your "no interruption" timeframes, close your office door at work to reduce uninvited visitors.
- Turn off social media notifications during high volume and peak work hours.
- Check email at set times throughout the day.
- Avoid self-interrupting behaviors such as multitasking. According to Gloria Mack, professor of informatics at the University of California, Irvine, 44% of interruptions are self-inflicted. Focus on one thing at a time.
- Remove "time buster" apps and programs from the home screen on electronic devices.
- Use a daily calendar system for time management. Share important dates with key individuals to reduce scheduling conflicts as well as to establish clear boundaries for how you intend to maximize your time.
- While the list of strategies centers heavily on digital disturbances, it is important to consider all types of opposition that hinder winning. Also keep in mind that there are moments when we are our own biggest opponents. This is where fear and self-doubt creep in.

In essence, we must recognize that opposition can be a person, place, thing, attitude, state of being, or a mindset. We are less likely to succumb to failure when we are able to accurately identify our oppositions and then strategize accordingly, even if we are our very own roadblock to begin with.

Mindset

It is imperative to discuss the influential power of mindset in this chapter. Mindset is everything when it comes to success and is even more influential than talent. In *Talent Is Overrated: What Really Separates World-Class Performers From Everybody Else,* author Geoff Colvin says, "The best performers set goals that are not about the outcome but are about the actual process of reaching the outcome." So, while talent is notable, having the necessary skills, mindset, and vision to execute is essential for every success story. While most recognize that their ways of thinking are closely connected to their worldview and decision making, more attention should be given to how our mindset can be the ultimate factor in dictating whether we win or lose. A winner's mindset acknowledges that through whatever adversity, success is inevitable. According to Brian Tracy, we are able to change our lives by changing the way we think. Having healthy mental habits is the fortitude that keeps us going during difficult situations and helps us land on winning. When considering some of the greatest athletes: Serena Williams, Lebron James, Muhammad Ali, or Lionel Messi, they all demonstrate a relentless winner's mindset.

Optimists Are Limitless

One of the most valuable mental habits to combat any type of opposition is optimism. Optimists are goal driven individuals who typically think about what they want in life and how to achieve it. Unlike pessimists, optimists are void from deficient thinking and see the opportunities life has to offer. As a person thinks, so is he or she. So, if healthy mental habits are cultivated, positive thoughts will ultimately become the harvesting ground for winning behaviors. However, a winning mindset isn't simply handed to you and doesn't become inherited only by reading about it. A winning mindset must be developed and refined over time. According to Forbes, a winning mindset is built by several factors: not relying on your talent, building your grit, generating momentum with small steps, trusting your vision, and taking action.

A winner's mindset isn't for the weary or the faint of heart. For example, former WNBA superstar turned entrepreneur Swin Cash believes winning mindsets include mental toughness and emotional resilience and often exclude other people's thoughts or opinions. "A winning mindset doesn't allow the shortsightedness of others to deter them from being great," she says. "Those with a winning mindset have faith in their vision and are mentally tough. Nothing great or worth having comes easy."

While we know that winning is about maneuvering effectively through opposition, you can ultimately learn anything you need to learn in order to achieve your aspirations in life. The only real limits are the ones you place on yourself. Motivational speaker Les Brown once said, "To achieve something that you have never achieved before, you must become someone that you have never been before." This quote does not suggest morphing into your inauthentic self; however, it does convey the importance of personal self-development in order to refine your skills, talents, and craft.

It is with a winner's mindset that you will be able to overcome most, if not all, opposition that comes your way. Overcoming challenges builds character, character-building leads to small victories, and over time ultimately leads to big wins. As you consider your opposition, answer the questions below to set you on the path to strategizing for your next win:

- What or who are your opponents in life?
- What strategies, habits, or goals can you establish in order to combat your opposition?
- What distractions are getting in the way of attaining your desired goals?

- Consider your top five. Of those individuals, who would be a good thought partner to assist in strategizing against opposition in your life?
- Are there any self-interruptive habits you have created? If so, how will you develop new habits?
- Do you typically have an optimistic or pessimistic mindset?
- How has your mindset either contributed to or hindered your success?
- How would you describe your winner's mindset?
- What is your natural response to opposition, adversity, or difficult situations? Is there anything you would like to change about this response?
- How do you typically study (or pay attention) to the opposition in your life?

Do Now Exercise

Based on your current goals, create a list of your top five oppositions and explain why each exist. Create a plan for how you will minimize or eliminate each opposition. Lastly, be sure to allot for needed resources, time, and key individuals.

Chapter Review

- We must recognize that opposition can be a person, place, thing, attitude, state of being, or a mindset.
- When it comes to winning in life, it is imperative to identify factors that are stifling your growth and then dig deep in order to get to the root causes.
- Winning is about being able to identify and mitigate all distractions hindering growth, progress, and success.
- One of the most valuable mental habits to combat any type of opposition is optimism.
- Possessing healthy interpersonal and relational skills are such huge components to winning.
- The only real limits are the ones you place on yourself.
- Establishing reasonable and realistic boundaries is necessary in order to keep interruptions and distractions at bay.
- A winning mindset is built by several factors: not relying on your talent, building your grit, generating momentum with small steps, trusting your vision, and taking action.
- The shortsightedness of others should not deter or weaken the faith and vision you have. It should fuel it.
- Overcoming opposition builds character. Embrace the opportunity to become better.

"My best skill was that I was coachable. I was a sponge and was aggressive to learn."

– MICHAEL JORDAN
SIX-TIME NBA CHAMPION.

CHAPTER EIGHT

You Win By Remaining Coachable

The idea of coaching has primarily been a western concept developed in the United States of America. In 1875 Harvard and Yale played one of the nation's first football games recorded in the history books. Yale hired a head coach by the name of Walter Camp, and he positioned the team to win 26 out of the 30 games played over three decades. Walter Camp was not only smart, but he was also wise enough to bring in assistant coaches who would become position coaches for individual sections of the team. He established practice schedules, performance records, and a game plan for each game. After decades of defeat Harvard got wise and also hired a coach.

When we think of the climate of today's sporting arena, we would never think of a team without a coach. The reason for this is that the sporting world has discovered that there is always room for improvement. Coaching subscribes to the mindset that we are always "becoming" and will never "arrive." There is always room for improvement. Ironically, this is not the pervasive mindset of many industries or fields. For many jobs or career paths, expertise is expected upon completing a college degree. The span of control for your growth and development is through your own efforts the rest of the way. The coaching model challenges this status quo and reminds us that improvement through coaching is a way of life.

Coaches Are Farmers And Editors

A coach's primary goal is to maximize the potential of the coached. When you think of a coach consider them as a farmer or an editor. A farmer puts the seed in the ground and must have the patience and wisdom needed to cultivate and sustain the growth towards maturity and eventually fruit bearing. A farmer's mentality is to grow the product. Their job is to create the conditions for the plant to thrive. This is also the role of a coach.

Coaches are also like editors. An editor is a critical reader who polishes and refines a writers' work. Editors focus on the details such as fact checking, spelling, grammar, and punctuation. There are times when editors help guide the clarity of thought by cutting and focusing the writers' work. A coach's job parallels the idea of editing the efforts of the coached. The coach's role is to continuously improve clarity and performance in those being coached.

Becoming Coachable

Becoming and remaining coachable is by far one of the most vital ingredients for winning. Many people view coaching as a deficit because they don't understand the role and purpose of a coach. Many think a coach is needed because an individual is not good enough or has fallen short. This kind of thinking is usually fueled by pride. Being coachable requires a level of exchange. One must give up their personal agenda with the trust that another individual will lead them to greater attainment. This process is not easy, nor does it come naturally for many. For some, they must tear down the wall of fear and replace it with dependency and trust.

To become coachable there are six areas to consider:

1. **Be Humble:** Being humble requires admitting and accepting the fact that you don't know everything and that you need help to get better. If we are not growing, we are complacent,

and complacency is the enemy of progress. When we are not coachable, we lack the humility needed for exponential growth.

2. **Be Willing:** A huge component of being coachable means you have a desire to learn from others. When you have a desire, it burns naturally from within, no one has to force you. A forced will produces the character of a rebel, so it is critical that your drive comes from your desire to be better.

3. **Be Respectful:** Respect has to deal with value. The things we value we respect and the things we respect we value. Being coachable means you place value on the process and the person who is coaching you. They have the skills you want to acquire, so give them the respect of your undivided attention. Being coachable means, you are willing to try something different and put your full effort into making it work for you.

4. **Be Vulnerable:**
Vulnerability gives you permission to be human. Humanity begins at the point of vulnerability because we have permission to admit when we are not good at something or when we need help in a particular area. Vulnerability allows us to open up in ways where we are able to receive the guidance needed.

5. **Be Accepting:** Being accepting means having a willingness to receive feedback and critique. This disposition is easier for some than others. Without humility, willingness, and respect, becoming accepting can be challenging for many. Being accepting is a sign of mental and emotional maturity. You non-defensively recognize that growing involves harnessing the power of corrective coaching.

6. **Be Great:** Greatness is a mindset. The lion is considered the king of the jungle not because it's the biggest, tallest, strongest, fastest, or even the wisest animal in the kingdom. The lion is the king of the jungle because he simply believes he is, and the other animals do as well. A major part of being coachable is believing that you are going to be great as a result. The word

believe is made up of two words: live and by. What we believe, we live by. If you are told to be ready by 7 p.m. because you are going to be picked up by a friend, your belief would be reflected in your actions. If you don't believe your friend is coming to pick you up, you are most likely not going to use the effort to get dressed. Beliefs drive behaviors. Believe that remaining coachable will make you great and it will happen.

Vantage Points

Coaches provide vantage points we cannot see. They are able to offer insight and observations that we don't understand, nor are able to see outside of ourselves. The Johari Window is a perfect example of this. Coaches can develop the four sides of this window. The Johari Window is a concept developed by two psychologists, Joseph Luft and Harrington Ingham in 1955, and is used primarily for self-awareness. According to this concept, everyone possesses four sides to self.

> When we remain coachable, we leave a door open for constant growth and maturity.

The public side: that's the side of us we show publicly. The private side: that's the side that only a few intimate people know. The blind side: that's the side others can see, but we ourselves cannot. The undiscovered side: that's the side that we and others can't see.

The beautiful thing about remaining coachable is that you will be able to develop the sides of the Johari Window, especially the blind side. Remaining coachable allows the opportunity for our blind side to be developed exponentially. It's hard to change what we can't see or don't know. That's why we need a coachable spirit. One of the single most effective methods to winning is receiving feedback. It is often said that feedback is the breakfast of champions. They eat it every day. Feedback then becomes your first daily meal. Remaining coachable allows you to be feedback rich. Being feedback rich allows winners to develop a level of expertise in a much shorter time span. Expertise in any area is the constant adjustment of behavior based on feedback.

When we remain coachable, we leave the door open for constant growth and maturity. A coachable person is a growing person. They possess what we call a hungry mindset. Hunger is defined as having an intense craving, a compelling desire. Being coachable also means having a growth mindset. It places us in the continuous improvement model where we are always seeking ways to develop, enhance, modify, strengthen or simply put, get better.

Better Faster

A coachable person will get better faster. Coaching allows you to simply grow faster by leveraging the expertise, guidance, perspective, know-how, and experience of another. This in turn allows us to break through the limiting beliefs we hold and propel us toward the goals we desire. Think about the coaching influence of Benjamin Braham on Warren Buffet, a very successful and wealthy businessman. He needed a coach. Without Epictetus, Marcus Aurelius wouldn't be one of the greatest philosophers, general, and emperors of Rome. Without Mike Krzyzewski, the Duke Blue Devils men's basketball program would not be as successful as it has been over the last 38 years of his leadership.

Good coaches multiply talent they don't diminish it. When you think of a coach look at them as "intelligence multipliers." Coaches who use their intelligence to magnify the intellectual capacity and talent of people around them are multipliers of intelligence. They are able to create exponential growth through what researcher Liz Wiserman, author of *Multipliers*, calls the five core assumptions: 1) They see genius in others; 2) They create intensity that requires best thinking; 3) They extend challenges 4) They debate decisions 5) They instill ownership and accountability.

According to Atul Gawanda, a medical surgeon and writer for *The New Yorker*, "A coach is your external eyes and ears providing a more accurate picture of your reality. They recognize the fundamentals by breaking down your actions and then help you build them back up again." Coaching is centered around growing and making improvements. When we remain coachable the sky is the limit. Everyone needs a coach.

Do Now Exercise

Think about someone who sees your blindside more than anyone else. Ask them to identify two to three areas where you can improve. After receiving the feedback, find someone to effectively coach you in improving in those areas.

Chapter Review

- Coaching subscribes to the mindset that we are always "becoming" and will never "arrive." There is always room for improvement.
- The coaching model challenges the status quo and reminds us that improvement through coaching is a way of life.
- Coaches are also like editors. A coach's job parallels the idea of editing the efforts of the coached. The coach's role is to continuously improve clarity and performance in those being coached.
- Being coachable requires a high level of vulnerability. One must give up their personal agenda with the trust that another individual will lead them to greater attainment.
- Coaches provide vantage points we cannot see. Remaining coachable allows the opportunity for our blind side to be developed. It's hard to change what we can't see or don't know. That's why we need a coachable spirit.
- One of the single most effective methods to winning is receiving feedback. Remaining coachable allows you to be feedback rich. Being feedback rich allows winners to develop a level of expertise in a much shorter time span.
- Coaching allows you to simply grow faster by leveraging the expertise, guidance, perspective, know-how, and experience of another.
- A coach is your external eyes and ears providing a more accurate picture of your reality. They recognize the fundamentals by breaking down your actions and then help you build them back up again.
- Everyone needs a coach.

"You learn more from losing than winning. You learn how to keep going."

– MORGAN WOOTTEN
FORMER HIGH SCHOOL BASKETBALL COACH

CHAPTER NINE

You Win By Working Hard And Never Giving Up

Winners are resilient. In the face of adversity, they don't just bounce back, they bounce forward. Oftentimes the best lessons are learned through failure rather than through success. Resilient individuals are able to look at life through the lens of growth and opportunity and use their perseverance as a motivating guide. The taste of success is hardly ever reserved for those who aren't willing to work hard. The reason most don't achieve their goals and dreams in life is because they either allow fear to keep them from getting started or they give up too soon. While working to complete a very difficult task, a wise man once advised us not to quit because the finish line was probably much closer than we realized. Working hard coupled with focusing on the intended outcome is a recipe for success.

Hope Is The Secret Ingredient

Hope is the great fuel that fires the engine of never giving up and working hard. Hope causes us to reach beyond what we can see and pushes us toward new possibilities and endeavors. It is directed toward what we don't possess and rooted in what we desire. This is why hope fuels the energy that keeps us pushing on.

The Australian speaker Michael Frost gave a compelling talk about

Vienna, Europe, during the period leading up to WW2. He talked about three Jewish psychiatrists, two were masters in the field, and the other a young, upcoming apprentice. The first master was a man named Sigmund Freud. He spent years studying people, striving to understand what makes us tick. He reached the conclusion that the most basic drive in human beings is the drive for pleasure and our need for pleasure explains why we do what we do and how we live. The second master was Alfred Adler. He too spent years studying human behavior. His studies led him to disagree with Sigmund Freud. Adler was convinced that the bottom-line explanation for human behavior was power. Many live their lives feeling inferior and powerless. According to Adler, life is a drive to gain control and to feel important. The third man was a young up-and-coming psychiatrist by the name of Victor Frankl. He hoped to follow in the footsteps of his mentors, but before his career gained any momentum World War 2 started. The Nazis invaded and it became dangerous for Jews. Freud and Adler were world-renowned scholars and managed to escape before Hitler invaded; however, Frankl was not so lucky. He was arrested and thrown into a Nazi concentration camp for four long years.

After the war was over Frankl was released from the concentration camp and resumed his career. While reflecting on his time as a prisoner, he noticed something quite strange – the people who survived were not always the ones you expected. Many who were physically strong wasted away and died while others who were much weaker physically grew stronger and survived. Why? What was it that enabled them to hang on through a living nightmare?

Frankl reflected on the theories of his mentors. Freud's pleasure principle couldn't explain it. For four desperate and terrible years the men in that camp knew only pain, suffering and degradation. Pleasure was not a word in their vocabulary. It wasn't pleasure that kept them going. What about Adler's theory about power being the basic human need? That didn't fare well either. Frankl and his fellow Jews were completely powerless during their time in the concentration camps.

Each day they stared down the barrel of a loaded gun, were treated like animals, and felt boots on their faces. They had no power nor any prospect of power.

Victor Frankl came up with his own theory. The difference between those who survived and those who perished was **hope.** Those who survived never gave up their belief that their lives had meaning. Despite everything going on around them, they believed the torture would one day end and they would then live meaningful, purposeful lives. What is the basic human drive? What is the one thing that gives life value? The ability to live with a sense of meaning and purpose. Not pleasure. Not power.

The lack of hope is the death of mankind. A hopeless man is a defeated man. At some point we have all been students. Imagine what you would do if your teacher told you that you had no chance of passing their class no matter your efforts? When the hope of success is stripped away, the inevitable result is to give up. We shut done and withdraw our energy. When you take hope away, you take life away. As long as there is life there is hope, you must remember that.

Self-Discipline Is Key

Perseverance is defined as persistence in doing something despite difficulties or delayed success. Persistence is self-discipline in action and perhaps one of the greatest examples of self-discipline is the ability to push through when the going gets tough. Self-discipline is the internal ability to do what you should do, when you should do it, without coercion. This level of disciplined behavior requires an inner strength of character coupled with a determined mindset. This drives individuals to follow through with their commitments, even after the excitement or enthusiasm have subsided. In essence, winning individuals commit to paying the price repeatedly until they have reached their goal.

This is reflected in the success story of Orison Sweet Marden, author of *Pushing to the Front.* Marden was plagued by the Great Depression and lost everything he had. Inspired to rebound, he rented a room in a stable and was inspired to write a motivational book to inspire others to persist in the face of difficulties. Marden wrote tirelessly every day for one year. On the eve of the completion of his book, he decided to go into town to grab a bite to eat. While away for dinner, the stable suffered a great fire and he returned only to find that his entire manuscript had been destroyed in the fire. Determined to persevere, Marden spent another year re-writing the book. After rejection from multiple publishers, one company gave him a chance. Marden's book, *Pushing Forward*, eventually became the nation's best-selling book and was touted as the leading influencer for helping businesspeople and politicians make key decisions in advancing America forward. Without Marden's perseverance and self-discipline to rewrite his book, *Pushing Forward* would have never been written, nor would it have had an impact on shaping the growth of the United States.

Grit

Angela Duckworth, author of the book *Grit*, talks about her journey of coming up with the theory she now holds about talent, effort, skill and achievement. According to Duckwork's theory, talent multiplied by effort equals skills (talent x effort = skills) and skills multiplied by effort equals achievement (skill x effort = achievement). In other words, talent is how quickly a person's skills improve when they invest effort. On the other hand, achievement is what happens when a person takes their acquired skills and use them. What she discovered is that if you take two individuals from similar circumstances, what makes the difference in their achievement will be driven by two things, talent and effort.

Talent is important; however, when you look at Angela Duckworth's theory you will quickly notice that effort is a two-part implicator. It's implicated with skill and with talent. To simply put it, there is nothing like "never giving up". Effort matters in all situations and frankly has the ability to close the gap between others who possess natural talent or skill. The reality is our IQ, natural talent and even our genes are not accurate predictors of future success. At the end of the day your grit or never giving up mentality, is a huge indicator for success.

Become a Completer

Successful people are completers. They find ways of getting things done through effort. Think about this for a second. If you are in college, trade school, or even the military what matters most is finishing. You must complete. If you are working on your doctorate, you must complete! The secret to success is learning to be a completer and this is where two-part effort plays a huge role.

Sometimes we overestimate what we can do in one day and underestimate what we can do in several days. If your intended outcome is to lose 20 pounds and to run in a 10K don't underestimate the point of small efforts over consistent time. Eventually, that daily walk can turn into a daily jog and that daily jog can turn into a daily run. Before you know it, you've developed enough grit to sustain a 10K and enough habit-forming power to lose the desired weight. Always remember that today's walk is better than the run you never did. Never give up! Winners consistently work until the very end. Whatever you are working on, commit to completing it and then keep at it with tenacious, unwavering, effort.

Look at your challenges as an opportunity to grow in grit. Consider them a blessing that prepares you for the next level. When we come to understand that our ability to learn is not fixed and can change with effort, it changes our limitations and our response to challenging situations. Consider grit as muscle that grows through effort. Never giving up will cause you to grow in ways that you could never imagine.

Learning to Persevere

Perhaps one of your greatest assets is your ability to keep at it, even when things get tough. James Corbett, one of the world's greatest heavyweight boxers said, "You become a champion by fighting one more round. When things are tough, you fight one more round." For those with ingrained self-discipline, this tenacity comes naturally. However, it's not so easy for others. What many may not understand is that perseverance is a skill that can be developed. Just as one can strengthen their physical agility, perseverance can be strengthened over time with the appropriate life experiences and wisdom gained from those experiences. Having the necessary skills is vital to the journey of success. While working hard consistently is imperative, working efficiently is of even more importance. This idea is reflected in the popular statement that we ought to work "smarter and not harder." This is where knowledge and wisdom become imperative to the destiny of success. With each victory gained along the way, we should be mindful to retain lessons learned so that the gained knowledge can be applied to future successes.

> ## Winners consistently work until the very end.

Oftentimes the acquisition of knowledge, wisdom, and skills is not considered and can be the greatest factors to sabotaging your success. Ultimately, we must remember that winning is not a destination, but rather, it is a process. And it is through the process that we become more and more refined. Those who are successful hardly ever focus on the end goal, instead they live by wholesome guiding principles that ultimately work in their favor. In essence, successful people don't pursue success, they pursue rules and principles. In return, success is the byproduct or outcome of a disciplined life that is grounded in principles associated with success. It's simple. Winning is associated with the principle of cause and effect. It's proven that whatever effort is put into any given task, will produce a synonymous and sometimes even greater output. With that being said, winners work hard and never give up because hard work and perseverance over time eventually lead to success. The ability to push through in spite of adversity is a winner's quality. Hopefully you find the poem below by an anonymous author as a source of inspiration as you continue to push to your next level of success.

Those who are successful hardly ever focus on the end goal, instead they live by wholesome guiding principles that ultimately work in their favor.

When things go wrong, as they sometimes will,
When the road you're trudging seems all uphill,
When funds are low and the debts are high,
And you want to smile but you have to sigh,
When care is pressing you down a bit,
Rest if you must, but don't you quit.
Life is queer with its twists and turns,
As every one of us sometimes learns,
And many a failure turns about,
When he might have won if he'd stuck it out.
Don't give up, though the pace seems slow –
You may succeed with another blow.
Often the goal is nearer than
It seems to a faint and faltering man;
Often the struggler has given up
When he might have captured the victor's cup,
And he learned too late, when the night slipped down,
How close he was to the golden crown.
Success is failure turned inside out –
The silver tint of the clouds of doubt,
And you never can tell how close you are –
It may be near when it seems afar;
So stick to the fight when you're hardest hit –
It's when things seem worst that you mustn't quit.

Author Unknown

Consider the questions below as you continue on your journey to success:

- What motivates you to work hard?
- What success principles guide you on a daily basis?
- Have you mastered the art of chunking your big goals into small attainable tasks?
- What does perseverance look like in your life?
- What are your strengths when it comes to persevering? What are your weaknesses?
- What areas are you wanting to give up on? Why?
- Have you created a timeline with realistic and measurable goals to keep you motivated?
- Who is your accountability partner to keep you motivated when you feel weary?
- Does fear and self-doubt play a part in you wanting to quit?
- What new habits can you adopt to keep you self-motivated?

Do Now Exercise

Consider your goals. Do you envision any challenges that may hinder reaching your goals? If so, write them down. Next create a game plan for how you will tackle these challenges if they arise. Be sure to include key people who can assist. Completing this task will allow you to be proactive rather than reactive.

Chapter Review

- Winners are resilient. In the face of adversity, they don't just bounce back, they bounce forward.
- Resilient individuals are able to look at life through the lens of growth and opportunity and use their perseverance as a motivating guide.
- The lack of hope is the death of mankind. A hopeless man is a defeated man.
- Self-discipline is the internal ability to do what you should do, when you should do it, without coercion.
- Self-disciplined behavior requires an inner strength of character coupled with a determined mindset. It drives individuals to follow through with their commitments, even after the excitement or enthusiasm have subsided.
- Winning individuals commit to paying the price repeatedly until they have reached their goal.
- Effort matters in all situations and frankly has the ability to close the gap between others who possess natural talent or skill.
- Whatever you are working on, commit to completing it and then keep at it with tenacious, unwavering, effort.
- Successful people don't pursue success, they pursue rules and principles that they live by.
- The ability to push through in spite of adversity is a winner's quality.

"He who has a why can bear any how."

– DR. VIKTOR FRANKL
HOLOCAUST SURVIVOR

CHAPTER TEN

You Win By Focusing On Something Bigger Than Yourself

When considering the above quote by Dr. Frankl, the "how" and the "why" serve very distinct roles. The "how" are the strategies for getting the work done in achieving your goals -- but without knowing the driving reason or the "why" behind it, you will have a difficult time staying on track, no matter how great the strategies are. Think of the "how" as the engine -- it will make movement happen and move you forward. Whereas the "why" is your fuel to keep you going. All great sports teams, coaches, and athletes arrive at and maintain their winning streak because they are driven to success by something much greater than themselves. The late, great, basketball coach Jim Valvano is quoted saying, "A person does not become whole until he or she becomes a part of something bigger than himself or herself." Whether that is competing for the greater good of the team or for something more personal, most successful athletes step into greatness because they understand their place and greater purpose in this world. The same is true for highly successful people in other arenas of life, outside of sports.

Pause for a moment and ponder this question – Why do you do what you do? What is your compelling why? This is an essential question because it is the driving compass for everything we do. Understanding your "why" gives purpose to your life and will motivate you past any adversity. It is also crucial to understand the direct correlation between purpose and success. Success is not measured by the number of stars, accolades, or dollar signs; however, it is instead measured by one's ability to live out their true purpose or calling in life.

Levels of "Why"

According to Dr. Andrew Shatté, we are driven by four levels of "why":

- **Level 1: Individual goals.** At this initial level individuals are concerned on a personal and individualistic manner mainly with their material possessions, financial attainment, career advancements, and personal achievements.
- **Level 2: Family.** Level two takes your why a step beyond yourself to include the people closest to you. At this level individuals are not driven by their own self-centered pursuits but are rather motivated to do more for their family.
- **Level 3: Community.** At this level individuals are driven not just by their own achievements or the well-being of their family but are also motivated to influence the world around them. At this level, the perspective is more so "big picture" where individuals are motivated by a purpose bigger than their own personal agenda and welfare.
- **Level 4: Religion, spirituality, values.** Individuals at this level are connected to something larger than themselves and are typically driven by the very highest level of achievement, greater than the people around them. Their compelling why may be rooted in God, spirituality, or a set of values they live by. In short, individuals at this level are legacy-driven and are looking to make an impact in ways that will outlast and outlive them.

Dr. Shatté goes on to say that the higher the level, the greater your resilience. Each level of purpose causes a deeper reach as to why we are compelled to do what we do. The greater the purpose; the more grit is needed to persevere through the highs and lows. However, before you can fully understand what level your compelling "why" resides, you must consider your thoughts about the notion of winning being tied to purpose. Winners don't simply win for the sake of winning. Winners win for bigger and deeper purposes that can't exactly be seen or measured on the field or court.

> The greater the purpose; the more grit is needed to persevere through the highs and lows.

Over the past seven years we have experienced exponential growth. However, after taking an inventory on how we've spent our time, treasures, and talents over the last soon to be decade, we concluded that our wins have been primarily inspired by our desires to help and serve others. As educators with bleeding hearts to help others, perhaps it just comes naturally. But ultimately, it was not the career advancements or salary increases that led us to write this book, start a nonprofit, or officially brand our marriage mentoring business. Our compelling "why" has and continues to be our fuel for the fire lit inside of us to make lives better for others. We simply believe that when we help others win, we win too.

If you're wondering about your purpose as you are reading this, ask yourself these simple questions. What adds meaning and satisfaction to your life? And what is it that gives you a sense of purpose? Understanding that winning is tied to something greater than yourself is not only a good thing, but it is also healthy. Studies show that having a sense of purpose is an increasingly strong predictor of happiness and a powerful antidote to depression. Research also indicates that 'purpose driven' people:

- Are four times more likely to be highly engaged in their work.
- Are 50% more likely to be a leader.
- Have 64% higher levels of career satisfaction.
- Typically earn a higher income and have a higher net worth.
- Enjoy 42% more contentment overall.
- Typically live up to 7 years longer than other individuals who don't possess a sense of purpose in life.
- Experience reduced health risks such as reduced incidents of strokes and lowered risks for Alzheimer's disease.

While the benefits of living a purposeful life are obvious, finding one's purpose in life isn't always so easy. There's no instruction manual on how to live a purpose-driven life, however the proven strategies below can serve as a guide for helping you tap into your definitive purpose.

- **Pursue your passion.** Your true purpose to a winning journey must be rooted in something that you personally want and are passionate about. Your passion will fuel your efforts to reach your goals.
- **Define what's important to you.** So many people wander through life without knowing what's really important to them. Take a survey of your life by categorizing things, goals, and people into two categories: authentic and superficial. Be sure you are truly placing your priorities in their correct category. Sometimes we incite misplaced value on people and things without realizing that our energy and efforts should be appropriated to what's really important in our lives.
- **Be authentic to who you really are.** Unfortunately, some people struggle to find purpose in life because they don't allow themselves to be who they truly are. Instead, they try to adapt to other people's definition of life, thus creating a false sense of their reality. Additionally, they don't allow themselves to be who they truly are because of fear of rejection or criticism.

- **Be mindful of your inner critic.** Having a strong intuition or "gut feeling" can be a good thing when an individual is in tune with their purpose. However, self-inflicted criticism is a defense mechanism that oftentimes stands in the way of living a purpose-driven life. Silence your self-doubt by focusing on your passion and the skills you are equipped with to master your purpose in life.

- **Your purpose must be reasonable, achievable, and believable.** We've all heard the saying, "The skies the limit." While this can be super motivational, it is important to make sure your purpose aligns with your current reality and is in harmony with other goals, priorities, and responsibilities. According to Napoleon Hill, "There is one quality which one must possess to win, and that is definiteness of purpose, the knowledge of what one wants, and a burning desire to possess it." As you consider your true purpose, ask yourself; "What is my purpose and how badly do I want it?"

Below are a few additional guiding questions:

- What are you passionate about?
- If money were not a necessity, what path in life would you explore?
- What keeps you going every day? What motivates you?
- Based on this chapter, what is your current level of "why"?
- What is the one thing you would dare to do if you knew failure was not an option?
- What would you rate your current happiness level on a scale of 1-10 (1 = lowest, 10 = highest)?

- What barriers are holding you back from living in your definitive purpose?
- Does your purpose(s) align with the other significant areas in your life? If not, what changes will you make in order to create alignment?
- What thoughts about yourself do you need to change or eliminate in order to live a more fulfilling life?
- Think about your goals. What is your "why" and what is your "how"?

Do Now Exercise

Reflect on your big goals. Determine your "how" for reaching your goals and write them down. Next, determine your "why" for each goal and write them down. Lastly, ask yourself whether or not your "why's" are the driving force behind you reaching your goals. If the answer is no, do a re-evaluation as to why you have set the goals that you have.

Chapter Review

- Know the difference between "how" and "why". The "how" are the strategies for achieving your goals. The "why" is the driving force behind your goals. Think of the "how" as the engine -- it will make movement happen and move you forward. Whereas the "why" is your fuel to keep you going.
- Understanding your "why" gives purpose to your life and will motivate you past any adversity.
- Winners win for bigger and deeper purposes that can't exactly be seen or measured on the field or court.
- Understanding that winning is tied to something greater than yourself is not only a good thing, but it is also healthy.
- Studies show that having a sense of purpose is an increasingly strong predictor of happiness and a powerful antidote to depression.
- Your true purpose to a winning journey must be rooted in something that you personally want and are passionate about. Your passion will fuel your efforts to reach your goals.
- Unfortunately, some people struggle to find purpose in life because they don't allow themselves to be who they truly are. Instead, they try to adapt to other people's definition of life, thus creating a false sense of their reality.
- Silence your self-doubt by focusing on your passion and the skills you are equipped with to master your purpose in life.
- Your purpose must be reasonable, achievable, and believable.
- Ask yourself: What is my purpose and how badly do I want it?

About The Authors

Ovett Wilson, founder and CEO of R.E.F.O.R.M., is an expert in the field of education. His experience includes classroom teaching, mentoring, life coach, assistant principal, principal, professional development trainer, motivational speaker, and university instructor. Mr. Wilson is currently a principal in Tampa, Florida. With over 16 years of leadership experience in PK-12 education, Mr. Wilson has spent countless hours studying and applying effective practices to enhance performance and achievement.

Mr. Wilson has a passion for high-needs student populations and has a sense of urgency to bridge the expectation and achievement gap. Mr. Wilson was inspired to establish R.E.F.O.R.M. due to his strong desire to raise the bar in achievement, performance, and quality leadership. R.E.F.O.R.M. is a dynamic training that will shift your perspective in a manner that will motivate you to raise your expectations in order to advance student achievement.

Dr. Adrianne Wilson holds a B.S. in secondary social science education, a M.Ed. in educational leadership, and an Ed.D in educational leadership from the University of South Florida. With over 16 years in education at the K-12 and college levels, Dr. Wilson is currently a Professor and Coordinator of the newly developed Master's in Educational Leadership program at The University of Tampa in Tampa, FL.

As an academic researcher, Dr. Wilson's research platform includes the development of multiple disposition assessments for undergraduate teacher prep programs, educational leadership programs, and online learning environments. Her established research has landed a solid contracted partnership with Watermark, which has resulted in the adoption of her assessment tool in hundreds of institutions of higher education throughout the United States and US territories. In addition to her assessment work, Dr. Wilson is also an independent consultant where she provides diversity and inclusion training for local K-12 schools. Lastly, Dr. Wilson serves as co-owner and consultant for R.E.F.O.R.M.

Connect With The Authors

Website:
www.tenlawsofwinning.com

Mr. Ovett Wilson can be contacted at:
ovett.wilson@gmail.com

Dr. Adrianne Wilson can be contacted at:
dr.adriannewilson@gmail.com
www.adriannewilson.com